Between Two Bridges

by Victor Colaio

ISBN: 1-4392-1448-4
ISBN-13: 9781439214480
Library of Congress Control Number: 2008909358

Visit www.booksurge.com to order additional copies.

Prologue

When my mother brought me into the world in 1936, my body only knew to survive by breathing, seeking nourishment, and resting. Little did I know that the timing of my birth took me into a world of pain and sacrifice that had occurred in the past and would continue into the future. History has documented well the hurt and suffering of the worst economic depression our country would ever know. Awakening and attempting to rebuild from that tragedy, our parents and grandparents faced even more catastrophic sacrifice—World War II. However, these successive traumatic and lucid events of sacrifice gave this country a renewed sense of morals, ethics, hope, and, yes, a touch of genuine happiness.

While too young to understand the events that were taking place in my formative years, I was able to enjoy my teenage development in a state of happiness that had never occurred before and would never happen again. Happiness in its most pronounced state of well-being entered my life in the decade of the fifties. Anyone can argue that his or her childhood was filled with happiness. No one in this world can dispute or judge a person's contentment. What is clear to me, however, is the fact that when you grow up with less, you embolden your mind and emotions with imagination and hope. Sure, I suppose that fighting and wrestling almost every day in the streets from age eight to eighteen is not a formula for attaining happiness or success. Living on the Lower East Side in the 1940s and 1950s did not allow you to retreat to a confrontation-free sinecure. What life did was to enlighten you both mentally and physically to the meaning of sacrifice. It ignited your imagination and instilled in you a toughness that would guide and strengthen you as you dealt with choices and problems.

Growing up after World War II produced a feeling of happiness and relief after a period of darkness. Hope exuded as we held block parties for those returning from war. This sense of renewal gave us kids a lift. We all seemed to have a future. As we grew as teenagers, we all worked after school or during the summer—shining shoes, cutting blueprints in sweatshops, loading vegetables on stands, carrying ice, or working on the docks or in the Fulton Fish Market. No one had cars, bicycles, or expensive sneakers. Very few had televisions or even telephones. Distractions were few. Some teenagers fell in love, as Butch and Margaret did, and raised a beautiful family. Contributions from the Lower East Side were many, starting with Governor Alfred E. Smith, U.S. Senator Jake Javits, Attorney General Lou Lefkowitz, and Jimmy Durante. Our neighborhood produced a Catholic priest, a famous rock-and-roll singer and several professional baseball players. Some of us went on to college, many to work on the docks and at printing presses. The scars of the Depression encouraged multitudes to take civil service jobs.

When the time came for us to enter adulthood, we took with us not only dreams and hope, but memories of extraordinary happiness. Whether it was Pete the Lash standing on the ledge of the roof twelve stories high with flashlights turned on him to see if it was really King Kong...or the belly treatment administered by the big guys, or playing tackle football with a rolled-up newspaper and no equipment.

There was nothing more positive and supportive in experiencing this extraordinary happiness than our own immediate families. My mother, grandmother, aunt, and especially cousins Beverly and Vivian...all our families gave us the support and experience of life, but more important—their unqualified love.

We grew up in innocence, but quickly learned lessons in the streets. The year 1957 was coming to an end and, as Paul and I were awaiting our call-up to active duty with the U.S. Army, we came upon the destruction of our neighborhood. Through eminent domain, our buildings and churches were being demolished in order to build a huge private residential cooperative complex and a new police headquarters.

We clutched each other's shoulders and, with tears falling, we knew then that life would never be the same. The pureness of our happiness would be forever tainted by the change of the 1960s. The distractions and human character failures would prevail into the twenty-first century. We were blessed at least, in our youth with the greatest decade of happiness that America ever enjoyed, despite our lack of material possessions.

Many of our neighborhoods are gone, but we were blessed by God for the period we grew up in. Those of us who remain cherish those moments of happiness and remind each other that true happiness on earth is not the future, but rather in remembering the past.

Dedication

This book is dedicated to Mark and Stephen, my best friends, my pals, and my loving sons who perished on September 11, 2001. My wife of forty-five years, Mary Christina, who emigrated from Ireland to marry me and become the foundation of my life and family, my daughter Jean, whom I love without qualification and who inspired me to write this book. My five grandchildren, Delaney, Max, Joseph, Catherine, and Sophie, who give me the buoyancy to remind me that life is good. My brother Jerry, who provides me my moral compass and always remains close to me.

Victor Colaio

Acknowledgements

Many thanks to my friend Charles Bennett Grubb for his layout and editorial suggestions and for his extraordinary help in computer skills not given to this author.

A very special thanks to photographer Gail Soodek for her vivid and spectacular pictures of my old neighborhood, including the two bridges that cross the East River, which defined my formative years.

A tribute to my editor for her outstanding and impressive talent in making me look good. The editor, of course is Gail Cato, and she is indeed the best of the best.

Between Two Bridges

I am told it was a hot summer night when I was born. It also happened to be the night Max Schmeling knocked out Joe Louis. My father's emotions were somewhat mixed since his first child and his love for boxing seemed to have collided that night. Nonetheless, the firstborn child of Ferdinand and Jean Colaio started his developmental years on the Lower East Side of New York. My fate would be a tenement apartment, small and dark, on a block called James Street. The streets in the neighborhood were named after famous Englishmen like James, William, and Oliver. There were also streets named after American presidents such as Roosevelt, Madison, and Monroe streets.

My early years did not register well in my memory. Suffice it to say that a very emotional incident arose while living on James Street. My dad brought toys home as often as two to three times a week. One night he brought home a stuffed dog that I promptly named *Queenie*. She was a nice fluffy and cuddly dog and we slept together every night. One day, for a reason unbeknownst to me, Queenie was lying on the window ledge. The window was open and, while I could never imagine my dog lying on a windowsill, I was not concerned. After all, we all need a little fresh air. As I continued to play with my toys, I happened to look up and noticed Queenie was missing. I became very concerned and summoned my father to help me find Queenie. Since the window was open, Dad looked out only to discover Queenie lying at the bottom of an air shaft. He immediately ran down to the grocery store where he alerted the owner. Imagine the owner's reaction when told that a small puppy had fallen out of the window. While slicing, the startled owner leaped over the counter and pushed through the back door only to find a stuffed dog missing one eye.

"Geez, Freddy, you nearly gave me a heart attack," was his first reaction.

Queenie and I were reunited, but unfortunately I could not find her eye.

I was too small to remember anything very uneventful happening on James Street. However, in 1940 my mother was pregnant and Dad felt we needed a nicer apartment. Sure enough, we landed in a rather new building. The apartment on Madison Street was sunny, bright, and it was tiny. It also was on the top floor of a four-story building. This fact gave us a very good and very bad situation to either enjoy or decry. A top-floor apartment meant an easy few steps to the roof for hanging clothes and sunning yourself on *Tar Beach*. It also meant every time we went shopping we would have to lug groceries up four flights.

The building was the melting pot of all melting pots. There were Italians, Irish, Jews, Spanish, Greeks, Slavs, French, Russians, and Germans. The occupants were so varied in vocation you might consider the building a tourist hotel without a concierge. You had civil servants, wise guys, bookmakers, bartenders, dock workers, craftsmen, and clerks. You even had a doctor who made house calls. These people voted as Democrats, Republicans, and, in one instance, Communist.

The vocations were indistinguishable because in this apartment building, as in many apartment buildings, all doors were open during the summer months. People would invite each other for coffee or dinner. No locks, no bars, no gates; a free-air zone permeated by pungent food odors. European visitors to our apartment building would think they never left home—with the exception of the Lower East Side accents. The hospitality was next to perfect. I often think of those very times when I would climb the four flights to my apartment only to be tranquillized by those intoxicating odors of foods and seasonings, sauces, pot roasts, garlic, peppers, gefilte fish, cabbage, and coffee. With all those odors exploding in the hallways, infusing the clothing on my body, no one could ever fault me for my voracious appetite.

Chapter Two

Mom gave birth to a beautiful little girl named Linda. She had beautiful brown eyes and curly brown hair. I loved my little sister and did not mind giving up my crib for a folding bed in the living room. This would be my resting place for the next eighteen years. Horrible conditions prevailed during this time period. Daily papers would tell us about the war in Europe and then the attack on Pearl Harbor. The radio was filled with news on both fronts. It appeared that everyone was leaving the neighborhood. All the young men were disappearing as the draft was collecting them by the dozens. Many sons would never come back. Those who did seemed never to be the same. Many came back in flag-draped coffins and many with missing limbs.

They limped and they had hooks and wooden legs. Our neighborhood boys had worked to protect freedom. These were the same sons who experienced their parents' anguish, pain, and loss of self-esteem during the terrible Depression. If ever there was a profile in courage, it was the parents who lived through the Depression and raised their sons for World War II.

Never in the history of the United States was there more euphoria and excitement as there was at the end of World War II. The spirit and camaraderie of our country's citizens reached a pinnacle never to be attained again. It was our greatest moment, especially in the cities. There were block parties and welcome-home parties. The unification of families solved all problems. The problems of the world were now ended. It was as if God had given us a new beginning and amazingly these soldiers and sailors never talked about their experiences. They'd done their job.

Chapter Three

In 1941, I started school in the first grade at St. James Grammar School; this, the same school that was attended by Alfred E. Smith, our former governor and first Catholic presidential candidate. It was an old school, but very clean. The nuns were like all nuns; they dwelled on discipline and order in the class. They were also loving and understanding. For example, one day I had an accident. I urinated in my pants, but stood silently as my urine flowed down my leg onto my shoes and finally the floor, forming a miniature lake beneath my feet and those of my classmates. They suddenly discovered it was me. I was mortified but Sister Mary Gerard hugged me and called my mom. Sister Gerard understood how much I hurt at that moment.

Life was pleasant at St. James. We studied our arithmetic, our history, and our penmanship. We showed our adoration for the Blessed Virgin, especially in the month of May. We practiced Catholicism as it should be practiced, via the Baltimore Catechism. For some very strange reason, the classrooms for me represented an open space for imagination and a connection to what I saw in the movies. American history classes focused on the forty-eight states from the time of the Pilgrims to President Roosevelt. The description of the West always fascinated me, as I could only imagine states like Texas, Oklahoma, the Dakotas, Montana, and Wyoming—huge plains run by cowboys and lit by brilliant skies. How the hell else could a kid on the Lower East Side visualize the rest of the United States? The farthest I had been as a kid was Staten Island to the south and Van Cortland Park to the north.

Chapter Four

My sister Linda and I were pretty comfortable in our new apartment. As I retired each night, my folding bed felt great. A wire structure held together by springs and hooks with a mattress so thin you could feel these hooks and springs embedded into your back. It seemed a small price to pay just to be alive and living in America. By the way, this folding bed would forever be known as a *Bronda*...which is northern Italian dialect for a folding bed.

The concept of sleeping on a folding bed was not only practical but also interesting. The bed was used only in the living room, which was approximately 10 ft. by 12 ft. including the foyer. I would awake to the pungent odor of urine excreted by the large community of alcoholics and homeless who wandered south of the Bowery. The Bowery attracted misfits, alcoholics, disgraced physicians, and professionals who, through human error and decadence, had failed in life. They were attracted to similar characters and lived in fleabag hotels in the Bowery. Sometimes they would pass through our neighborhood to beg for money to purchase additional alcohol. The El pillars, some twenty feet from my building, were great repositories for urinating, not only for animals but for humans unable to hold it any longer.

On a hot summer day these odors would engulf the neighborhood. In contrast, the internal odors would exude coffee, stock broths, fish, gravy, stews, and sometimes the sweet smell of basil. Consider, after all, the attributes of this poor neighborhood. Italian and kosher butchers who sold you every cut of meat, including sweet hot sausages, pork products, and kosher meats, cut, trimmed, and seasoned to perfection. The fish stores were like aquariums of dead fish, although you would on occasion see some of these creatures crawling. Fillet of sole, bass, porgies, gefilte fish, white fish, shrimp, calamari, scungilli, clams, mussels, and oysters. Fresh fish from the Fulton Fish market every day. Add to these foundations of life the vegetable store, which was really the market, with beautiful lettuce, tomatoes, parsley, basil, cabbage, cauliflower, watermelons, peaches, plums, apples, oranges, tangerines, cantaloupes, and honeydew melons. Last, but not least of course, these gardens of paradise would supply us with our fresh cut Christmas trees.

The other emporiums of taste and smell were the delis. The Italian delis with their salami and cheeses, their peppers, pickles, and salads, not to mention the glorious scent of parmigiana cheese. Complementing these products of paradise were small *Manhattan Specials,* which contained coffee and root beer, and for those older, the choice of local beer like R&H, Rupert's Knickerbocker, Piels, and Schaefer. I believe every man before he dies should have a hero sandwich of Genoa salami, provolone cheese, and roasted peppers on crisp Italian bread—a euphoric combination! The Jewish delis were even more pungent; after all, who could pass by the smell of pastrami, corned beef, or brisket? Place them on rye bread with a pickle and mustard and one could start to believe he or she was on the very top of the world.

Life, however, did not end here. No citizen of the Lower East Side could ever forget our bakeries. Crisp and crusty Italian loaves and the birthplace of focaccia as we know it. It is legendary that the finest focaccia bread was made on Roosevelt Street, where citizens from all the wards would come to buy it. The only peril, however, was the proprietor, who enjoyed his wine so much he often left the focaccia in the oven too long; he delighted in his libation. The scent of this bread was extraordinary. Like others, I would lean out my window and absorb the smell. This was focaccia made to perfection. The formation was not too thick, but a tad crusty with olive oil over its distinct ridges. You could place many combinations atop this specimen but most people's preference was dipping it into coffee. The Italians from the north described this as *tucca*, i.e., to touch.

The pastries were even more descriptive. You had cannoli, pastachottis—tasty cookies topped with pignoli (pine nuts)—and rum babas, not to mention the artistic cakes with all their calories. Some bakeries offered lemon ices. These were cups of crushed ice saturated with lightly salted lemon. Like all specialties, this delight was made by a proprietor on Roosevelt Street who surpassed all of his competitors. The lemon ice was all he sold and they came and they came and they came. The test of superiority was the fact that these lemon ices were so delicious that literally many of the cups they were placed in would also be devoured. The lust for more and more was insatiable. The passing of that proprietor brought much sadness to the neighborhood, leaving behind those empty wooden barrels that served as the memorial to the quenching of thirst.

Finally, no block would survive without the candy store. Just think of the *charlotte russe*—sponge cake and real whipped cream topped with a cherry. How about those jelly apples covered with jelly syrup shining in your face? Those candy stores were actually enablers to addiction. Loose cigarettes, known as *loosies* were available for those of us who tried to smoke and did so until caught by our parents. Those who did not get caught, I would bet, are still smoking today. A big favorite among the local gentry was seltzer, milk, and Fox's u-bet chocolate syrup (an egg cream); once tasted, you were hooked! One candy store was better than the other. For those less inclined toward sweets, you had a *two cents plain*, a straight up seltzer water. Variety was a trademark of these stores. Besides the great newspapers like *The Journal-American, The News,* and *The Mirror,* you also had marbles—round objects that served the city kid very well. After all, the streets were the entertainment vehicle to the youth at that time. Oh, those marbles...the *regular,* the *puree*...and, of course, the steelie. And there, in the middle of it all, an olive distributor scenting our activities on our beloved Roosevelt Street.

Chapter Five

After getting comfortable in our new apartment, I started meeting new friends and schoolmates. At the age of five I began living two lives, one on Roosevelt Street and the other on James Street, the home of my grammar school. None of my classmates lived on Roosevelt Street except Catherine, who lived in my building, and George, who lived in 14–16. Most lived in their fashionable Knickerbocker Village apartments, an interlocking community of high-rises that took up one square city block. It was behind *The Journal American,* so many of its occupants worked in the newspaper industry. Others came from the *hook,* a neighborhood east of our school.

St. James Grammar School was in the shape of a triangle; across the street was St. James Church, which became the pillar of our community. Besides operating a parochial school, it served as a bastion for social events including dances, bingo, novenas, and, of course, Sunday Mass, where all would attend, dressing up for their hour of faith and obligation.

Leading the congregation of the faithful was Arthur Gerard Keane, a very visible and vocal priest, remembered most for his very, very short temper. Just ask any altar boy serving mass with Father Keane about their embarrassing moments. I would see my classmates serving as altar boys receive a slap to the face for some minor infraction during Mass. Imagine their humiliation and embarrassment—remember this was the 1940s and part of everyday life. In retrospect it did no harm, but rather enforced discipline and conditioned us for life regardless of social or political correctness. It was a different time. Those who suffered would later become successful because they understood discipline and authority.

Perhaps a better assessment of Father Keane was his generosity. I had always thought that priests represented material poverty, that they lived off the generosity of their parishioners. Father Keane was not in this category. I discovered he had come from a wealthy family; after all, who could own a beautiful new green Cadillac in 1947? I later found out that priests educated and ordained by the archdiocese were not subject to a vow of poverty. The very authoritative and stern Father Keane had a generous heart. Those same altar boys he slapped also enjoyed a ride in his car to his parents' home in New Jersey where they would cool off from the sweltering heat of the streets and be treated to a swim in the lake and a sumptuous picnic lunch. This was, after all, a priest—a servant of God—who tried his best to serve and demonstrate Christianity.

Because of its connection to the school, St. James Parish had many activities in which parishioners could participate. One of these was the St. Patrick's Day Dance, an event held annually at Webster Hall on East 11th Street. Everyone would attend dressed up to the nines! Many parishioners participated in the entertainment segment of the evening. It was a great opportunity to demonstrate your self-esteem, confidence, and more importantly the reality of oneself. In short it was a celebration of reality and human life. The desire to look good, feel good, and be good. Both parents and children attended this affair and it was always good to see the many sides of people.

St. James had a profound spiritual effect on my upbringing. The required Mass attendance every Sunday, the adoration and procession of Mary in the month of May, the Lenten sacrifices before Easter, the frequent use of the confessional as a reminder of our sins. This was the foundation of faith that helped me prepare for life with confidence and spirituality and served to reinforce my understanding of mortality and human frailty. Perhaps the most memorable event of Christianity and compassion came to me in the form of an associate priest assigned to the parish. His name was Father Wilders. He had shocking blue and penetrating eyes. I recall falling one day in the school yard, and hurting myself. I had scraped my knees and was bleeding. As my mother was attending to me, Father Wilders came over to offer his help. He leaned over and began to clean up my wounds. I looked straight forward into his eyes and could see them swelling with tears. He felt bad for both my mom and me. To see the face of this priest was to see the face of Jesus. His genuine concern for another human being demonstrated the Christianity that I had been taught. How ironic that a priest assigned to St. James demonstrated so beautifully the work of God. I was told later in life that this priest not only performed his duties in a priestly manner, but also in a saintly manner.

Chapter Six

In class I could see very clearly that women would one day succeed as well or better than men. When this might occur, I didn't know. However, throughout my grammar school days, the girls in the class were much smarter than the boys. Not only were they pretty, they were intelligent. Maureen, Jackie, Jacqueline, Theresa, Barbara, Catherine, Barbara V., Roseann, Ethel, Marjorie, Consuelo, Marie, Ann Marie, Jeanie, Mary Jane. There was also Elizabeth, who had a physical disability, but was as smart as the rest. The boys were represented, but not as many. John, Dickie, Smithy, Joe, Frank, Jo-Jo, Anthony, Billy, and Georgie. I remember that in the early part of my grammar school days, a couple of the boys were disruptive and had to leave. Little did I know that many landed in jail. This was, after all, a very tough neighborhood. There would be little hope for the meek.

The nuns were a great source of education and inspiration. God love them; they were devoted teachers and sisters in every aspect of the word—religious, but not oblivious to the ways of the world. Our neighborhood abounded with schemes and debauchery. Ours was not a pristine community high on a hill, surrounded by trees and lakes. This was a community of concrete and tar. It was filled with canyons of darkness and light. It provided basic, but often crude facilities for living, both bitter cold and sweltering hot. There's a saying that the climate of the Lower East Side guided the behavior of its citizens. Suntans were obtained on the roof amid the hanging clotheslines and the smell of hot tar. Tar Beach, as the roof was known, also served as a delightful respite from the sweltering heat at night. Where else could one enjoy a lighted skyline while lying on the fire escapes, absorbing the soft crosswinds of the East River? The bitter cold of the winter brought with it outdoor fires and shacks built by the neighborhood boys, mostly on desolate Hague Street. Heating in buildings was almost nonexistent; blankets, sweaters, and more blankets were the items for winter.

Back to the nuns. In the year 1943, as the Great War raged, I was sitting in a third-grade classroom listening to Sister Bernadette instructing us in art. For some reason, unbeknownst to me even now, I began to draw the rudiments of an ape. The gorilla family always fascinated me...I guess it was my trips with Dad to the zoo...but I decided to draw a penis on the ape. Since this was an art class I imagined this would have some intrinsic value. On the other hand, this was 1943 and my teacher was a Catholic nun. I decided to pass this masterpiece to my classmate Anthony, under the desk. Sister caught this act and asked to see the paper. This was the most traumatic event of my life at that time... surpassing pissing in my pants in first grade. A Catholic nun had been exposed to my vulgarity in the form of art. My mind raced over the consequences. Would it be expulsion? Would my parents be notified? Perhaps a visit to the principal's office—most likely a beating at the hands of Sister Bernadette. Alas, none of the above...Sister took me out of class and asked if I was sorry for what I had done. Without delay I admitted to being profusely sorry, and received the standard punishment..."I must not ___ ___ ___" one hundred times. God bless Sister Bernadette.

Chapter Seven

Attending school and learning from the nuns was a fulfilling experience because in conveying and teaching the subject matter, the nuns captivated the class when describing parts of our country. Your imagination would wander to the West when Sister would talk about our American history, the Lewis and Clark Expedition, the Indians, Seward's Folly (the purchase of Alaska), and the Louisiana Purchase...cowboys and the gold rush to California. In a classroom on the top floor of St. James perhaps thirty boys and girls would imagine what life was all about. For me, I would dream of the great sky and the Rocky Mountains. Thoughts of an abundance of fresh air and open land were very appealing in contrast to a dark classroom in the shade of the Third Avenue El. All of us were trying to reconcile what America was really like and how our living in walk-up tenements affected our perceptions. Fresh air and tranquility were not environmental elements that existed then for us. They existed only in history books.

Why then were we reluctant to be the pioneers our parents and grandparents had been? Was it the euphoria of being among families who loved their children without qualification? These same parents were always present during the day to dress, wash, clothe, and feed us. To counsel us and kiss us. To make sacrifices for us in order to educate us. Perhaps it was the food and culture that seemed to talk to our bodies and souls. We had Chinatown, Little Italy, as well as the largest Jewish population in the city. Our Spanish, Greek, and Slovak neighbors added their contributions. What an abundance of riches. You had all of Manhattan, the Battery, Wall Street, City Hall, the museums and zoo at Central park, Rangers, Rovers, the Knicks, the football Giants, and the later the football Yankees and Dodgers, the baseball Giants, Yankees, and Dodgers too. To hell with the fresh air of the mountains. We had our own dreams to fill right there on the Lower East Side. I, for one, would always dream of Mom's dinner. Pasta fagioli, risotto, or maybe a juicy steak. I could not imagine getting these staples in Wyoming. I was wrapped up in a blanket of many cultures, all of them warming my heart and mind and stomach. And school was great. You had one teacher for each grade and developed an appetite for knowledge. You learned penmanship, religion, math, English, history, and reading all from one teacher. It was great.

I enjoyed my schoolmates, but really did not associate with them outside of school. This was because of geography. You see, kids never really left their block to play. There were several reasons for this. The prime reason was that we had to be under the watchful eyes of our mothers. They had a wonderful vantage point. They could stand outside their buildings or look out of fourth-story windows and see the entire block. The other reason was there was too much to do. Stickball, stoopball, Johnny on the pony, ring-a-levio, kick the can, football, marbles, pinochle, brisk, and craps.

Chapter Eight

By the time I was settled in at 11 Madison Street, my folding bed seemed more and more comfortable each night; this bed served me well for over eighteen years. My parents and sister, Linda, slept in a tiny bedroom. Linda was around four when, upon general examination, she was found to have leukemia. To everyone, Linda was a beautiful child. She had big brown eyes, skin as smooth as an onion, and very curly hair—not tight curls, but rather wavy ones. I loved my sister very, very much. She was a happy child and Mom always had her in a dress. I especially loved her in the velvet dresses that were trimmed with lace, but as beautiful and happy as this little girl was, she was always pale. My grandmother always said that you could determine people's health by the color in their faces, especially their ears. Linda lacked color. Her paleness, however, accentuated her beautiful brown eyes and glorious smile. Mom and Dad's little angel was dying. You could see Mom's terrible suffering, her hair turning white by the minute, even at the age of thirty-four. Dad had a slightly less frustrating life. His police department duties during wartime necessitated a sixty-hour workweek with no overtime pay. He was in the Emergency Service Unit at this time after spending fourteen years in two tough precincts, namely the thirty-second in Harlem and the eleventh on the Lower East Side. He genuinely loved his job and talked about it all the time. When you consider that my father took the police department exam at the height of the Depression, competing with tens of thousands including lawyers, engineers, and other college graduates, this was a major accomplishment for a young man who finished only the eighth grade. Good civil service jobs were diamonds in the rough. These were indeed very painful and harsh times; a civil service job was sacrosanct. At this time there was even a measure of social status attached to it.

Chapter Nine

Every Sunday, Dad would visit his mother and father at 60 Mulberry Street and as always in my family, the apartment was located at the top floor. Here is where Grandma Marie Soldaveri and Grandpa Vito Colaio came after they emigrated via steerage from Salerno, Italy, landing at Ellis Island. Their dream had been fulfilled. All their children together now, Americans, in the bright sunshine of their apartment overlooking Columbus Park, named after another famous Italian.

It was tradition that every Sunday all sons and daughters would meet at Grandpa and Grandma's apartment and discuss everything going on in the world. The apartment was actually quite nondescript. Suffice it to say that it was a typical railroad apartment, starting with a fire escape, a combination living room and kitchen with a bathroom to the side, approximately 120 square feet down the hall into one bedroom and then a second bedroom and finally a rear fire escape. As you proceeded from the kitchen to the rear of the apartment it would become darker and colder, almost 10 to 20 degrees colder.

On Sundays the ritual of the family took place at Grandpa and Grandma's place. All the cousins were present and accounted for. I loved my cousins. Angela, Juanie, Victor, Vito, Grace, and Grace. We shared our happiness with each other as well as with our uncles and aunts. Seeing, hugging, and kissing one another was not the crowning moment of the Sundays though. It was Grandma's sauce that really attracted all these flies. The smell of her Napolitano sauce with pork and meatballs was sheer joy. There was an aroma so distinct that your nostrils absorbed it like a sponge. Thick red sauce engulfing meatballs with all the secret ingredients bursting into a crescendo of aroma and flavor. The problem on Sundays was that Grandma had several loaves of fresh, crusty Italian bread on hand. All would taste the sauce by placing the bread in the sauce—called *tucca,* or touch—and the trouble was the sauce began to disappear...much to the worry of Grandma. Inevitably she had to make more sauce. She had been a beautiful woman with long blonde hair and remained lovely as she grew older. Grandma was quite a contrast to the typical southern Italian woman.

The sons, all bald except Uncle Johnny, would stand in the middle of the kitchen drinking whiskey out of shot glasses while daughters Anna, Mary, and Nettie talked among themselves and to their parents. On occasion, they would bring their husbands Uncle Julian and Uncle Pete. Aunt Anna, God love her, was a widow at an early age. Uncle Nick was the oldest and a bachelor. He was a longshoreman and had hands like hams and could crush Brazil nuts with his fingers. He had worked in ships' holds for years, loading and unloading cargo. He had fair skin and blue eyes and voraciously read newspapers, books, and magazines. He could tell you everything about the Wild West. He loved western stories. He was a warm and loving man who often carried me on his shoulders to the parks, especially all the way down to Battery Park. Make no mistake; Uncle Nick, although loving, warm, and compassionate, was a tough, tough guy. The only thing to be said was that he was a longshoreman and broke many a barroom jaw. A favorite story was the one of Uncle Nick visiting his favorite bar in the Bowery. While minding his own business, knocking down his customary whiskey shot, a rather tall Texan, said to have a gun, came into the bar. After a few drinks this big Texan became loud and boisterous and came over to Uncle Nick and threatened him. It did not take much in our neighborhood to respond to a challenge. Uncle Nick coldcocked this bastard with one crushing right to the jaw. It was said that this cowboy saw stars over Texas for many weeks to come.

Uncle Joe was the classiest of my uncles. He had the position of deputy postmaster in Manhattan's General Post Office and was a high ranking member of the Knights of Columbus. He was well respected in our community and always dressed well, wearing his famous bow ties. I was always thrilled when Uncle Joe came and drove us to a ballgame with his son Vito. Uncle Johnny was the most generous of my uncles. He always gave us quarters to buy ice cream. Uncle Johnny would give us the shirt off his back, literally. He was not blessed with fortune, however. His only daughter Grace was born with mental and physical deficiencies and to this day is institutionalized. Uncle John and his spouse Aunt Beatrice were good souls who did the best they could in this world. Despite all his problems, Uncle John remained happy, working hard and providing for his family. Though Uncle Nick was tough, Uncle Johnny, of all the brothers, was indeed the toughest. He feared no one and, if challenged, pity the other guy. Broad shouldered and big-handed Johnny boy, or, as he was known, Johnny Dooley, would crush you one way or another. God bless my uncle.

Uncle Mike, the only uncle to serve his country in World War I because of his age was most vocal. He had long arms and huge hands, a Colaio trait, and lived in Knickerbocker Village.

Uncle Mike was not blessed. He and Aunt Millie were childless. It was said that she conceived several times but the child died shortly thereafter. Uncle Mike and Aunt Millie were wonderful people, full of life and conversation.

Aunts Anna, Nettie, and Mary were very different in personality compared to their brothers, and amongst themselves too. Aunt Anna was the closest in age to my father and the youngest aunt. She had beautiful skin and lovely green eyes. As a widow, Aunt Anna had to go to work and raise a beautiful daughter, Angela. Like her brothers, Aunt Anna was a civil servant who cleaned the offices of the Supreme Court justices. Aunt Nettie was a registered nurse and was the most articulate and classiest of my aunts on my father's side. She was extremely clean and when we went to visit you could always expect a full place setting with napkins...even for a lousy salami sandwich! Aunt Mary, poor soul, was not blessed with stability. She had some nervous disorders that affected her life and, like Uncle Mike, was childless. But Aunt Mary was a good soul and had a wonderful sense of humor, despite her emotional shortcomings.

Grandfather Vito was a quiet man. He would sit in his rocking chair and take in the action, occasionally kissing his grandchildren. He had a full head of hair almost like steel. What a shame his sons were all practically bald. Vito Colaio had the classic attributes of manhood and epitomized the institution of marriage. Here was a man who left his native Italy with a wife and a gang of kids and settled in a virtual ghetto without friends or family. Can anyone deny that this was a profile in courage? Vito Colaio, a laborer, and father of eight children built our country not so much with his hands, but by his devotion to raising his family and as a volunteer maintenance man at his local church. Aside from six or seven hours of sleep a night, Vito Colaio worked each and every day of his life...no vacation, no sick days, no nothing.

All of Grandpa's children remember a very painful and terribly sensitive event. It took place sometime in the early 1900s. My grandfather entered a food store to purchase goods. He had difficulty speaking the language and tried very hard to convey to the storekeeper what he wished to buy. The storekeeper told him he didn't understand him and yelled, "Get out of here, you guinea greaseball, and don't come in here until you speak English!" This day would become a lesson to all of us...then, now, and forever. My grandfather, who was a genuine and wonderful Christian, did not get angry at the storekeeper. Rather he did something that has resonance to this day. He sat down with Grandma and his children and instructed them never to converse in Italian, but to speak only English. He and Grandma both spoke broken English, as tough and difficult as it was for them. The Colaio children spoke English only, read voraciously, and wrote with great clarity. How else could they compete and be successful? It worked and worked well. All the children got good jobs and advanced up the social ladder. This story exemplifies America and our success. Progress, progress, progress.

My dad continued to emphasize education at the evening dinner table. He often told us to be proud of our heritage, taste the food, dance to the music, sing the songs, frequent the feasts...but to remember that our true heritage was to be an American of Italian descent. We were Americans, and America came first!

Chapter Ten

Circumstances were getting very difficult because of my sister's illness. Her medical condition was deteriorating rapidly, and I, even at the age of eight, could see something was wrong. Suddenly, one day, Dad and Mom got dressed and began to dress Linda. I became apprehensive and my parents noticed my concerns. They explained to me that Linda would have to be hospitalized in order to undergo tests. Everyone was dressed and Grandma Domenica hugged me and kissed me and stayed with me while Mom and Dad took Linda to the hospital. My father held Linda in his arms and leaned over for her to kiss me. She immediately hugged me and gave me a kiss, and I hugged and kissed her back. Her cheeks were warm and smooth and for those few seconds it seemed we both did not want to let go. Two siblings inextricably tied to one another by blood, communicating for what would be the last time, their profound love for one another.

Little did I know that her imminent death would separate us forever. I would not see Linda again. Children were not permitted to visit the hospital. All I would remember was her angelic face and smooth skin and big brown eyes looking straight into mine. She moved her fingers indicating good-bye, still happy, at the age of four still exuding the innocence of a child. As the apartment door closed my tears began. I could see Grandma weeping at the window as well. My heart was cracking and my stomach turning.

"Oh God, why is this happening to my sister, an angel, child, and a life of purity and innocence? Why my family? Why, at the beginning and not the end of a lifetime?"

On January 6, 1945, the feast of the Epiphany, my sister Linda expired. On the celebration of Christ's birth, my sister Linda entered into God's kingdom, an angel of spiritual beauty and tranquility, nevermore to suffer, but only to enjoy the Kingdom of God and all the fruits of heaven.

My mother and father were grieving terribly. All arrangements were made with Bargicalupo the undertaker. Located on Mulberry Street in the heart of Little Italy, it seemed to attract as many patrons as did the bars and restaurants. There existed what I call professional mourners. People who would visit the funeral parlor almost on a daily basis and shed tears and agonizing cries as individuals left the casket to express their condolences to the survivors. These were very often old Italian men and women who would find respite in the warmth of a funeral parlor, scented with embalming fluid and floral bouquets. Dozens of mourners paying respects at simultaneous wakes held under the same roof.

It became apparent that many men did not cope with death as well as women. They would often retreat to a local bar and drink down whiskey. Coping with the death of a child would be more difficult. The sorrow was deep, the pain acute. On one occasion there was an elderly man named Bionding. He may have had mental problems and his visits usually brought apprehension. This time he had to be physically restrained. Crying out loud, he attempted to lift Linda out of the casket. Bionding was truly overwhelmed by Linda's death.

My mom and dad took me for the first time to view the casket. Each held my hand as we approached Linda. She was dressed in white, her tiny figure surrounded by flowers, emphasizing her angelic presence. Bleeding hearts, baskets, and bouquets all providing the ambiance of heaven. I knelt beside my parents, silently praying to Jesus, Mary, and Joseph, our Eternal Family, asking them to embrace my sister and give her joy and happiness forever. Her face was radiant, adorned by a tiny tiara, her tiny hands clasping a rosary resting comfortably forever. My parents were crying uncontrollably and I could feel their pain. The unthinkable of tragedies had happened. The loss of a child of five. Nothing could ever be the same.

Chapter Eleven

The year 1945 brought in a cold winter as my parents mourned their terrible loss. Something miraculous was taking place, however; my mother was pregnant and in April of that year my sister Anita was born. Another daughter and my mom and dad were extremely happy. It took their minds off the ever-consuming tragedy. I was also very happy and thanked God that I had another sister. Anita was beautiful, and like Linda had beautiful skin. Once again I had a sibling to play with; the void had been filled.

That summer my parents thought it would be a good idea for me to go to summer camp. Of course, this was unusual since it was prohibitively expensive magnificent luxury. No one from my neighborhood went to summer camp. Why should we? After all, we had fire hydrants, the East River, Tar Beach, and Battery Park for a few trees. What else could any good citizen of the Lower East Side ask for? Throw in some interesting recreational activities such as stoopball, stickball, a football made from rolled-up newspaper and twine, as well as multicolored purees and steelies. Wow! Worth mentioning too were the real big-time sports such as softball, played with the fabulous *clincher*, the hallmark of all softball. A real game of baseball had its great attraction because we could slide into the bases. This game was played exclusively in *the lots*...land situated directly under the Manhattan Bridge. It had a contemporary surface made of rocks, glass, nails, condoms, urine, and dog shit. On occasion we might deal with a body or a bolt flying off the bridge overhead. Sometimes a derelict from the Bowery who had perhaps decided to meet his maker.

My neighborhood would forever be destined to exhibit both misery and joy, a reminder to the rest of the country of the need to improve America. Mine was a complicated neighborhood made up of the poor, the repressed, and the downtrodden...yet, it was a simple life. You might choose your path and, as a street-smart kid, you had to learn fast. Nothing was easy and hunger was endless for some but we perceived life as simple and enjoyable and most importantly, hopeful. Why worry? God was good and our families loved us. We were clean, religious, and respectful. These were the qualities we always treasured.

Upon returning from summer camp, Dad informed me that it was affordable and that made him happy. I told my parents that the camp was very enjoyable. There was a lake and naturally all sorts of sporting activities. I told them that Sister Mary Louise, my fifth-grade teacher that year, took good care of me. She slept in a room adjacent to my ward, which was filled with happy campers. I'll never forget Sister Mary Louise. She was beautiful and had these gorgeous dimples. At night she would give me cookies and milk and had no shame playing favorites. She understood the pain my parents were going through and did everything to help.

In grammar school she was without question my favorite nun.

As I related my adventures to my parents I was eating plums, peaches, and bananas. My parents noticed that I had eaten close to a dozen plums and some three or four peaches and they cautioned me to take it easy or I might develop a stomachache. They were shocked to witness such a voracious appetite. Not too many months before they took me to a specialist to determine why I ate so little. Could it be that their baby had turned his eating habits around? Indeed, my food experience at camp solved the problem. Good homemade food, fresh fruit, and vegetables were a welcome event after years of frustration at the dinner table. My appetite would forever be changed by a simple stay at summer camp. Oh God! Thank you for blessing me with an appetite that all my parents, aunts, uncles, cousins, and grandparents had so eagerly awaited.

Chapter Twelve

After burying my sister, my parents' grief was now manifested in their daily lives. My mother was six months pregnant and that alleviated some of the sorrow. My father was transferred to a desk job in the police department after fifteen years as a productive police officer, thanks to his tough but compassionate Irish bosses. My father always respected the Irish, because they were generous in their help. Notwithstanding the abuse and discrimination my father experienced as a police officer because of his Italian descent, he tended to forget the complaints he received from the *shooflies* for obviously minor infractions such as a lunch period that was two or three minutes longer than allowed, or not being on post in below-zero temperatures. All now was forgiven because the good was surfacing in human nature and it was a time for healing. Mom and Dad now needed the comfort and support of my mother's family. They were very close to us.

The matriarch was Grandma Domenica Guarnieri who emigrated from Italy. Here was a woman I adored. Although she was my maternal grandmother, there was little difference in the love I had for both my mother and Grandma. Here was a woman who loved me more than anyone. At every opportunity she would kiss the cheeks off my face. When she woke me in the morning, which was often, she would kiss my feet as to gently start the awakening process. She could not do enough for me. One of the more satisfactory accomplishments was to wash my clothes, especially when my mother was sick. She was happiest when I came home from school or work to show me the whitest underwear neatly folded and freshly scented from the air that swirled around the rooftop clothesline. Here was a woman who as a child worked in the rice fields of northern Italy practically in servitude, but she had great love and devotion to her family and gratitude for merely existing in this great country of ours. She and Aunt Rose took over the responsibility of motherhood in a lot of ways— Grandma Domenica by her cleaning and Aunt Rose by her cooking.

Visiting my Aunt Rose on Sundays was a ritual that lasted for years. We all climbed the five flights at 17 Catherine Street, the birthplace of Jimmy Durante. This was an old law tenement building that held a dumbwaiter shaft in it. On holidays, especially Christmas, this apartment had the aroma of heaven. A litany of abundance included: homemade raviolis, kneaded and rolled for hours the night before, then laid on a bed sheet in one of the bedrooms. This particular bedroom doubled as a storage room because of its intensely cold temperatures. The warmth of the space heater in the living room dissipated before it hit the doorway. For those who had to sleep in this room there were four extra-heavy horsehair blankets available. Not to worry, however...more important the raviolis and their dough and cheese and spinach contents remained fresh. It was a great repository for Uncle Tony's homemade wine as well as all the other beverages. Not bad that apartment rooms on the Lower East Side were warmer or cooler based on location and not thermostats: front, sunny and warm; back, dark and cold.

Coming back to the kitchen, which served as the command center, Aunt Rose would rule despite the fact that her husband, Uncle Tony, was a professional cook. Aunt Rose would start the sauce early in the morning, with the help of a huge steel pot. Her sauce was truly, without question, the mother of all sauces. We, of course, referred to it as gravy. Starting from scratch you had the basic olive oil, garlic, onions, fresh plum tomatoes, red wine, some chicken broth, and, of course, the fortification of this concoction with the addition of braciola, pork and sausages. Aunt Rose had the secret ingredients always safely in her mind. Some guesses were salt, pepper, sugar, bay leaf, and other mysterious influences. The aroma intoxicated all who approached the apartment. You immediately got a high upon entering. The preliminary enjoyment started early with Uncle Tony serving everyone coffee royals, black coffee diluted with whiskey or anisette. Meanwhile, focaccia bread—square, oily, and crisp—baked in the oven. This was purchased at 10 Roosevelt Street where all would come to purchase the finest focaccia in the world. The custom was to dip the fresh focaccia in the hot coffee or, as we would say, *tucca.* Then there were those, including myself, who required a full breakfast. Eggs were not the order for Sundays; these were reserved for Saturdays. My primary nutritional breakfast was a large bowl of coffee, milk, sugar, and broken pieces of white bread and butter, called *seerpa*...closely sounding like slurping for obvious reasons.

The participants began filing in, Mom and Dad, my baby sister Anita and baby brother Gerard, who was born on Halloween in 1946, cousins Estelle, Ray, and their children, Diane and Bruce. The accompanying family of Aunt Rose, Grandma, Uncle Tony, Vivian, and Beverly were all present. My cousins Vivian and Beverly both had the most beautiful red hair imaginable. Colorists could never capture that shade if they spent millions. These were two beautiful red-haired young girls and my closest cousins.

As the day went on, we anticipated the arrival of our Uncle John and his wife, Aunt Mary. Uncle John, known in the neighborhood as *Red Egan*, owned a social café on Mulberry Street and served the customers, whose names were filled with vowels. He had no affiliation with these men other than to serve them coffee and liquor as they played ziganet and Greek rummy. These games would last well into the night and more likely into early morning. His arrival was dubious at best. His history told us that he would be awake perhaps two to three days consecutively in order to complete these games. By the same token, he was noted for sleeping two days in a row. He was very popular with his clientele, but more popular and loved by his immediate family. He was generous and loving. On special holidays he would always buy a large plant for his mother, Grandma. Delivery would be accomplished by a *stooge* paid $5 for his service.

Upon entering the living room one could smell the kerosene space heater and its warm fumes. A few more steps and there before you was a seven-foot, fresh-smelling, decorated Christmas tree, a tree always purchased by Uncle Tony at the eleventh hour on Christmas Eve for no more than $3. On Christmas Day, we would be joined by Aunt Rose's beautiful Jewish neighbors, Mr. and Mrs. Kreever and their daughter Evelyn, who was my personal math tutor. We all celebrated Christmas and Passover together.

Chapter Thirteen

Graduation from St. James Grammar School was nearing and this event initiated competition for awards at the end of the year for academic achievement. We had all kinds of contests to see who would be final winners. Written papers were submitted, spelling bees took place, math tests were given, and something that I found very interesting—a civics competition that involved immediate elimination. I loved civics and current events and even though I was the youngest to graduate the eighth grade, I was the last student standing. I was presented the award by my classmate Maureen's father who himself was in politics. It was the civics award. I felt something very special about this award because it represented knowledge about our federal, state and local governments that were served so well by those who were fortunate enough to be raised in my neighborhood.

Summer was coming and, as in recent years, my dad and mom, along with Uncle Tony and Aunt Rose, rented a bungalow in Midland Beach. This time we were closer to the beach and next to an Army Air Force installation called Miller Field. This required an armed MP to screen any pedestrian or vehicular traffic to enter. The MP was steps from our front door. Anita and Jerry were getting big and they really enjoyed the summer at the beach.

The months of July and August went by uneventfully with one exception. I do not know what happened, but my brother Jerry, who was almost five years old, became very angry at my parents and decided to leave home. Imagine, he had the wherewithal to jump on his bicycle and take off. My father was pleading with him to come back but to no avail. I saw what was happening and spotted Jerry's red hair moving behind a grove of green hedges. I jumped on my bike and chased him for over two blocks before I caught up with him. He was very reluctant to return home and I had a tough time convincing him that we all loved him very much. He was finally persuaded and Mom and Dad were relieved. Jerry was really angry and even at that young age had a mind of his own. Later on in life we would laugh at this episode.

Midland Beach was our first real encounter with suburban living with the exception of my summer camp years. It was quite a change to go from fishing for Spaldeens (pink rubber balls) in sewers to fishing for killies (tiny fish) or crabs in the streams of Staten Island. I rode my bike everywhere, which I could never do in the city.

When summer ended and it was back to high school I started to get somewhat apprehensive. My first year in high school required that I travel to 91st Street and First Avenue to an annex of Cardinal Hayes High School, via the Third Avenue El. This year I would have to go to the main building on 151st Street and Grand Concourse via the Lexington Avenue subway. There was a sense of excitement though, because I had gone to the main building a couple of years ago to see what Hayes was all about. I had been accepted to Hayes along with La Salle Academy and I was standby at Regis. Paul and I went to visit the school, and the glass backboards on their courts did it; this was the closest thing to playing at Madison Square Garden!

Chapter Fourteen

It was in the fall of 1950 and I was settling down in this beautiful *modern* high school built in 1941. The faculty was a very interesting mix of instructors. The most conspicuous teacher was a lay teacher, the only lay member of the faculty, excluding the physical education teachers and coaches. All other members of the faculty were from religious orders. Now, it is apparent to many people that members of the religious orders are probably the best-educated individuals of any group. Immediately, I came to realize that I, as a student, was the beneficiary of an abundance of knowledge. The faculty consisted of Diocesan priests, Franciscan priests, Xavierians, and Marist and Irish Christian brothers. When you consider the relationship between members of a religious faculty teaching young students, there can be no doubt about discipline. Many of us would shit in our pants upon the arrival of some of the priests and brothers. Silence was golden and prevailed in every classroom with few exceptions.

Every class was a productive, efficient, and absorbing process that eliminated any semblance of distraction or interruption. You learned your lessons with intensity and fulfillment whether through English grammar, literature, foreign language, religion, business law, or algebra. It is my contention, arguably, that my education at Cardinal Hayes was the equivalent of a general college program today. The reason for such a conclusion is that the absorption of knowledge and discipline in each class resulted in a successful transfer to a useful application of this knowledge to everyday life. Many today agree with my conclusion, I am sure.

Besides discipline, the dress code played a pivotal role in instilling a sense of self-esteem and seriousness. Jacket, tie, and white shirt, or course, was the uniform of the day. I got great wear out of my maroon corduroy jacket and the few white shirts that my parents could afford. It appeared that my timing was correct since I did not grow too much between the ages of thirteen to sixteen. My physical growth started during the ages of sixteen to nineteen when I grew two inches a year.

Life in high school presented a dramatic change in what I was used to in my neighborhood. The boys of high school presented a diverse population, different from the Lower East Side. In school, I saw blacks and Hispanics and a lot of Irish kids—and I mean a lot. They came from the South Bronx where many emigrated from Hell's Kitchen and Yorkville. There was also a group of Italian boys from Greenwich Village and East Harlem. The kids from East Harlem were very different in the way they dressed. Most wore *newspaper boy hats* and peg pants, but all wore jackets and ties. The high school attracted a lot of different boys from every part of the city. A majority came from the Bronx. This borough, while poor in certain areas, was also a bastion for middle-class families. Many of the students were blessed with families who owned homes and had backyards. Those who lived in apartments had ample quarters in clean neighborhoods like the Concourse, Bedford Park, Morris Park, Pelham, and Inwood. Many, however, lived in tightly knit neighborhoods in the South Bronx. Only a few of us came from Manhattan, a small percentage from the Lower East Side.

Traveling to Hayes for us was somewhat of an adventure. Paulie, Jackie R., and I had to take the Lexington Avenue line up to 149th Street and the

Concourse. This required a battle with the elements. From Madison and Roosevelt streets it was a full four-city-block walk in the rain, snow, and cold weather. No one had duffle bags or backpacks. You carried your books in a loose fashion, covered with brown paper bags, and marked by subject. Five and six books at a time. Any other method would make you a *sissy*. Besides your books, you had to carry a lunch. This, of course, was of utmost importance. Without this sustenance you were in deep trouble worrying about hunger. Mom always made a great sandwich and usually included a piece of fruit, and milk was always available at school. This was the best way economically to exist. Lunch money was too much of a financial burden. Tuition, after all, was $8 a month, a strain for my father.

On one occasion a vivid example of the importance of lunch was portrayed to its fullest. It was a rainy day and very cold. Not too many of us wore hats because we had to make sure our *dos* were satisfactory in case we met up with our female counterparts. If our hair got wet, it would be dry by 149th Street and then the saga would continue. On this day, my mother prepared a delicious sandwich made up of Genoa salami and provolone cheese on Italian bread, crisp and crusty. She wrapped it in waxed paper and placed it in a brown paper bag. As I was maneuvering toward the subway station at City

Hall, I had to make sure that everything was in place, books, lunch, and hair. As I approached the last big street to cross I set myself up for a dash to the municipal building where I boarded the subway. This street was called Park Row and the traffic was fed by the Brooklyn Bridge exit. The volume of cars on the street was always heavy. A traffic light was the only safety net in crossing. As I waited for this light to change, I often thought of what I could expect that day in school. Perhaps a test in American history, a new subject in algebra, or an oral Latin quiz. Seconds were precious, timing was everything. The light changed. I was moving quickly, almost running, and then the light began to change. I ran at full speed to cross, trying to beat the rain and the twenty or more cars ready to mow me down. Then it happened. My sandwich so nicely tucked in my brown paper bag slipped out as I ran. It was too late; the traffic was moving. However, I noticed my sandwich was not wrapped with the customary waxed paper. There in the street, my perfect sandwich opened up like a piss clam being squashed tire after tire, mortally wounded, abused, tortured, and seasoned with rubber. I stood, frozen, until I realized that my stomach was the most important issue and I needed to react. The light changed and the traffic stopped. I went back and picked up my sandwich, stripped of its protective brown paper bag.

There I picked up this mutilated gastronomic tragedy, wounded and smashed and showing no life. I placed it in my arm along with my academic tools and promptly got on the No. 4 line. Lunch came and I devoured my sandwich, rubber taste and all. Result? No ill effects. "Up Hayes and all its loyal men"...this was a time *For God and Country.*

Chapter Fifteen

Growing up on this block and going to St. James Grammar School was very different than the surrounding blocks. On Roosevelt Street, we had a very varied group of human beings starting from the upper part of the street, near South Street, where Governor Al Smith was born. Here we had a mixture of Italians and Spanish (those whose roots were in Spain). Roosevelt Street was split into three sections. This section had the toughest kids. Murphy, Doc, Avelino, Joe Fields, the Molach brothers, and Hammerhead. They controlled the block as well as Oak Street, which housed the old Third Police Precinct with authority. Nobody came on that portion of Roosevelt Street without meeting this contingent of mortals.

The middle portion of Roosevelt Street was more refined, although made up of only a few buildings. The population was Spanish with some northern Italians with names like Sanchez, Gonzalez, Bos, Varella, and Natiello. Hard-working families whose sons and daughters, while poor, would succeed in life through education. Their outlet was through sports. Two individuals on that block who excelled in athletics were Albino and Sergio—both super athletes.

The final portion of our block consisted exclusively of Italians from the areas of Genoa and Piacenza. This portion was the longest part of Roosevelt Street. Here we had several young inhabitants play professional baseball, a young boy who eventually became a priest, a boy who became a fifties singing star, and a Catholic Church that was the focal point of this particular block. This segment of the street started at the corner of Madison Street and St. James Place. On the east side was Frank's vegetable store, where fresh fruits and vegetables attracted many local residents. Across the street was my building with Pep's Bar, which at the time was the sports bar of the neighborhood with a large television. In the evening when the Giants played the Dodgers the place would be packed.

As I reached a double-digit age I began to infiltrate Roosevelt Street and mix with its inhabitants. The population was changing since many sons had returned from World War II. The block, approximately an eighth of a mile long, consisted of two bars, two delis, a pasta and ravioli establishment, two bakeries, a butcher, a wholesale olive oil importer, and, oh yes, an ice man, and that wonderful lemon ice merchant. Most prominently, however, situated in the middle of the block was St. Joachim's Roman Catholic Church, a church that had Italian masses and a wonderful hall for its social events.

My first encounter with my friends would be with Georgie and Mickey, all of us the same age but different in our views on life. In other words, a little weird at times, but we all felt compatible with one another. More importantly, we had great parents. We bonded nicely but had to be cautious because, while we all lived on the same street, we lived in different buildings; hence, we had to maneuver gingerly because every fifty feet there might be pockets of *older guys* who would congregate in their *spots* on the block.

These fellas, approximately five to ten years older were teenagers who positioned themselves in different locations. For instance, on the corner of Roosevelt and St. James Place, many congregated for purposes of advantage. You had a view of six corners and could view every female who walked by. A stoop on Roosevelt Street that accommodated card games and craps, plus a ready-made cement lip for stoopball located at the base of my building. This was a favorite of the *big guys*—Bobby C. and Joe L. They adorned themselves with tight-fitting shirts to exhibit their muscles, the peg pants (a sixteen was the size du jour), and blue suede shoes.

Down toward the midblock were Frankie Bull, Gino, and Andrew B., experts on Giant-Dodger baseball and bullshit artists supreme. Across the street antagonistic fellows like Joe L., Joe B., Jimmy C., and Danny F. were always lying in wait. Farther down you encountered Bopo and Bimbo, two brothers with great character and personalities who were always poised to break balls. Nearing the end of the block you encountered Roger Monk, Bobby C., and Charlie Lang for more abuse and perhaps some physical punishment. Interspersed were some nice fellows who had returned from the war and actually had career objectives: Al F., Johnny Tra-chi-mor—meaning *throw it here*—Paulie Knock-Knock, and a few others. These men would not participate in the daily abuse given out by the others, but amused themselves by watching as we grew up, eventually trying to sell us insurance and engaging in other forms of glee.

Chapter Sixteen

Our first encounter as friends was the Thanksgiving Day dress-up costumes. We all dressed as cowboys and took some pictures. Our first enjoyment together was the sport of marbles as we were too young to play stoopball and stickball. I remember Georgie having a couple of purees, marbles of pure color that had no markings. Mickey had a steelie, which was all steel, and a little larger than a marble. A steelie was worth five marbles, a puree two. It was interesting to manipulate a marble against a curb with a cobblestone street. If you could span two marbles with one hand, fingers extended you would win the marble. You could also win by *bombsies*.... i.e., drop your marble from a stand-up position.

Not too much time was given to marbles as we started integrating with the *big guys*. They needed players to fill their teams whether it was stickball or stoopball. That is when nicknames were created for all of us, as was the tradition for Lower East Side kids. For me it was Victor *Star,* to exemplify my ability in sports, for Mickey it was *Mouse,* obviously, and for Georgie it was *Egg Head,* for reasons unknown to this day

On a typical day when not in school we would get up and call to each other from the street. The *big guys* would congregate looking for a game. Stickball and stoopball in good weather, or football—two-hand touch—in winter. All the games were terrific because they had bets attached to them. What we needed was that pink ball, or *Spaldeen.* The stickball games were very interesting since on Roosevelt Street there was no wall with a chalk box. You could play the game with four, five, or six players on the field. The street was narrow; hence, you really had to hit the ball straight down the block. Of course, the sewer was home plate and each successive sewer indicated singles, doubles, triples, and homers. Each team had a catcher with a backup, usually the next batter. I always remember the talented pitching of Joe Lapi, Roger Monk, and Ray Bug. Roger even played professional baseball along with Bobby C. Bats were common broomsticks, some thick, some thin. You usually had an umpire, but if not, the catcher would call—a recipe for heated arguments. The umpire was usually a big guy who, in most cases, liked sports, but was not athletically inclined. We had incredible games and even though I was five years younger than everybody, I held my own. Fielding was my salvation. It created my nickname Victor *Star.* Stickball games were certainly more enjoyable than stoopball or punchball. What happened in stickball to this day is addictive. It created a fantasy environment. We had pitchers who actually believed they were in the majors, just by copying a professional's style. Ray Bug duplicated Robin Roberts with his precise curve ball. Joe Lapi thought he was Preacher Roe with his soft stuff. Roger M. pitched like the *Hondo Hurricane,* Clint Hartung—high, fast, and tight. The batters had dreams as well, some with stances like Willie Mays or Stan Musial while other copied the Duke or Mickey. We all had our fantasies, but these games gave us such happiness and provided us with such sweet memories. Ah! But the day was not done! Card games filled the latter part of the day—brisk, rummy, or pinochle. Maybe somebody bet a number or a horse, but cards were an integral part of our social makeup.

At night the activities were a bit more mischievous... ring-a-leavio, kick the can, or Johnny on the pony. Challenges were presented just about every night. Somebody or everybody had to use their hands. This led to sparring on the streets, or even wrestling down on the concrete. The *big guys* were notorious for constantly picking on us. They were bigger and stronger but I personally liked to mix it up. I loved boxing so much, and God gave me good hands—lousy feet, but good, big, nimble hands—and it gave me sufficient gratification to mess up the pretty boys' hair and faces with quick slaps to the face and head when we went at it.

Boxing was coming to a peak in the forties and fifties. Every Friday night was a thrill, with Gillette *Blue Blades* sponsoring the radio broadcast. The fighters were tough, good, and fought as often as once a month, moving from Sunnyside Gardens to St. Nicholas Arena to Madison Square Garden. All weights and classes had their champs, punchers, and punching bags, but the fighters were great. Marciano, Louis, Lesnivich, Walcott, Charles, La Motta, Ray Robinson, Gavilan, Basilio, Pep, Sandler, Fusari, Graham, Pallone, Terry and Paddy Young, Graziano, Zale, and my favorite, Beau Jack...the list goes on and on. No media hype for these fights, just good posters and announcements. Dad often brought me to see these fights and some of the beatings were brutal. Boxing, because of its frequency, became a subject of interest and conversation and actually beat out basketball and football in popularity perhaps because these sports were confined to a few large cities.

Chapter Seventeen

As things became tougher and challenges became more frequent, I noticed one day a new arrival on the block. It was not too conspicuous at the time despite the fact that a mother and her two daughters and three sons had arrived from Italy and moved into an old law tenement across the street. I later found out that the father, Bonfiglio, had emigrated from Italy a short time before and established a residence at 28 Roosevelt Street. The father awaited the arrival of his spouse and children after establishing himself. A short time after their arrival, however, Bonfiglio Gugielmetti died of a heart attack and left a wife and young family. This was a tragic event on our street and many neighbors mourned this sudden and tragic loss.

One day, as I was looking out my window on Roosevelt Street, I noticed a skinny kid in short pants running away from some of the *big guys*. He was super fast and he could move—speedy, shifty, and smart. They could not catch him. Where did this kid come from? I noticed him move frequently and it seemed that he was constantly being picked on. Now, it was easy to figure out his dilemma. Here was a kid who spoke Italian— with a dialect no less—wore short pants, and was the new kid on the block. This case called for absolutely no mercy and the *big guys* moved in. I saw this as another attempt on their part to control newcomers. It was getting obvious that the *big guys* were the whole show. We had to figure out how we were going to penetrate that life of games, girls, and being the kings on the block. I watched Paulie for a few weeks and saw a lot of physical talent. Besides being fast, he was agile and appeared to have genuine athletic ability.

I approached Paul one day and introduced myself along with Georgie and Mickey. Paul amazed me with the way he picked up the English language in such a short period of time. A fact that never left my mind was that while many families spoke their native tongue at the dinner table, they always spoke English once outside the door. The English language redeemed all of us as we progressed into the future. It was our most tangible connection to American culture. More than any other factor in our young lives, the English language introduced us to higher levels of competence and opportunity.

As I observed Paul, I knew he was a great kid and his kindness and good intentions were evident. It therefore became easy for me to take Paul under my wing, and so I did. I began to tell him that he could hang out with Mickey, Georgie, and me. We started to play ball together, then go to movies together, and always, always played games at night. Paulie was smart and he picked up baseball and football very quickly. As he integrated with us, the *big guys* gradually accepted him and it made it easier for all of us to get into the games.

Paul had a beautiful family. After the tragic loss of his father, his mother, Angelina, cultivated the family into a loving and compassionate unit. They had each other with a matriarch who, by Catholic Church standards, could very well have been canonized. It does not matter; in my mind she was a saint, just like all of our mothers.

The maternal relationship during the prewar and postwar periods was always the dominant factor in our lives. The theory was that the man was the horse who went out to the field to do the work for the well-being of his family, whereas the mother was always home to feed, nurture, educate, and care for the young. The watchful eyes of these women meant a foundation of family life with all looking to her for solid consolidation of the family.

Paul was only eleven when he arrived from Italy. His oldest brother Frank was the paternal figure in the family, complemented by his wonderful loving sisters Margie and Louise, who were always at their mother's side. In between Frank and Paul was brother John, who was the kindest and most loving of all. Frank was very sophisticated in his ambitions, tastes, and lifestyle. He divorced himself from the neighborhood and associated with friends uptown. This was a phenomenon during those times. Anyone who lived in our neighborhood basically limited their confines to a twenty-block radius for work, play, and all other cultural activities.

Paul, Mickey, Georgie, and I became very close friends as we carried out our daily lives. We all attended St. James Grammar School with the exception of Paul, who went to St. Joseph's. It was more of an Italian parish and I suppose more comfortable for Paul.

My relationship with Paul would grow every day as we had common likes and got along wonderfully. Of all the immigrants who established themselves in our neighborhood, his transition into our America was seamless. His command of the English language was rapid and without a trace of an accent. More important, his energy level surpassed anything we ever knew about living our lives. Here was a boy full of life and vitality who would energize me for decades to come. If I had to describe this energetic complexity, it would be that Paul was born with a hot pepper up his ass and there was no way to remove it.

THE AUTHOR-CIRCA 1939

AS A YOUNG BOY IN FRONT OF 11-15 MADISON STREET

STICKBALL-1953

EASTER SUNDAY-1954

READY TO RUMBLE-1955

ON LEAVE FROM THE US ARMY WITH GRANDMA-1958

LEFT TO RIGHT...UNCLE JOE, COUSIN ANGELA, VICTOR,
AUNT ANNA-8TH GRADE GRADUATION FROM ST. JAMES, 1949

ST. JAMES RC SCHOOL

LEFT TO RIGHT... EUGENE, MICKEY, RUDY AND
VICTOR-CHRISTMAS-1954

VICTOR, 8 AND SISTER, LINDA, 4 - 1944

ST. JAMES ROMAN CATHOLIC CHURCH

ENTRANCE OF ST. JAMES SCHOOL

PETER'S DELICATESSEN-STILL STANDING 2007

EMIGRANT SAVINGS BANK-WHERE ALL KEPT THEIR MONEY

MUNICIPAL BUILDING-WHERE WE PLAYED HOCKEY
AND KISSED THE GIRLS

GRADUATION ST. JOHN'S UNIVERSITY, NY-1957

LEFT TO RIGHT...VICTOR, GERARD, MOM, DAD
AND SISTER, ANITA, PARTIALLY HIDDEN

Chapter Eighteen

The heat of the night caused many strange things to happen in teeming neighborhoods. On our beloved block there were many young people from age ten to thirty, some returning from war, many with wounds and limbs missing, many in the seventeen to twenty-five bracket who controlled the block. Given the enormous and frequent physical activity of the days, the night became a reservoir for restlessness, because, weather permitting, the outdoors was our arena, most likely because the apartments back then were small.

Fun and relaxation were realized in different ways. In the middle of the block, there were oftentimes intellectual discussions on topics of social or political importance, but none were more heated than those involving baseball. Our block was divided between the

Yankees mostly because of our Italian population and Joe DiMaggio, as well as Rizzuto and Berra. Georgie and I were Giants fans and our day was coming in 1951. We suffered and supported our Giants, with Danny Gardella, Ernie Lombardi, Johnny Mize, Buddy Kerr, Wes Westrum, Hoyt Wilhelm, Johnny Rucker, and Hooks Iott—Say hey, Alvin Dark, Sal the Barber, Eddie Stanky, Mueller the Magician and Monte. They were all coming, these new breed of N.Y. Giants.

A lamppost was strategically placed on the corner of Roosevelt and St. James Place. This was the congregation point of the *big guys*. With Pep's Bar and my building across the street, we could hear the scores from the games. The opposite corner was a bus stop where people got on and off, across St. James Place was a clam bar, and across from the lamppost, a deli. The *big guys* dressed up at night and fantasized about the girls—some coming from work, some coming to buy lemon ice, some just walking by the boys. The dress code was predictable in the late 1940s and early 1950s. As mentioned, tight shirts, some were Ts, some silk, but always tight for muscle demos. Pegged pants were the rave with 16" peg the exact and proper tailoring for effect. Peg pants are narrower at the cuff, the narrower the peg, the tighter the cuff, with the 16" peg being the most popular size. The *coup de grace* was the blue suede shoes. These outfits were embraced, allowing those who wore them to feel like virtual supermen on the block.

The younger guys, however, thought they were getting the beatings and unwelcome attention; this had to stop. Strategic plans were now underfoot and a war zone was being constructed...invasion was inevitable.

Chapter Nineteen

The summers on the Lower East Side were simmering hot. Everyone sought out the night for relief. One summer night, Georgie, Paulie, Mickey, and I were ready to roar. This particular night we decided it was time. We all chipped in and purchased a dozen eggs—the arsenal was taking form. We now needed to decide from where we might launch these missiles for maximum effect. On the popular corner of Roosevelt Street under the lamppost, there stood this magnificent crowd of young men with tight shirts and peg pants. Bobby C., Joe Lapi, Roger Monk, Charlie Lang, Richie Igor, Gino, and Frankie Bull. Speaking of bull, the bullshit was so intense that the lamppost was clouding up.

We had to act fast and decisively. The problem was not one of attack, but one of escape. Once these eggs hit their mark, all hell would break loose and the roar of attack would rival that of Hannibal as he attacked in the mountains. Our strategy would be to immediately release and run in separate ways. We also needed to be close enough to hit our targets. We decided to launch from Gasoline Alley, which was an extremely narrow street dissecting Madison Street and Chamber Street. Each of us had three eggs, two in one hand and a third in our throwing hand. Paulie called the signals...on three. "Ready? One, two, three!" Egg attack one, then two, then three. These eggs hit with devastating damage. Yucky suede shoes, splattered silk shits, and ruined pegged pants. The *big guys* were stunned but not enough to fail to recognize their attackers. The hunt began. Angry and furious, the *big guys* now had inflamed tempers. Who would dare to destroy their images? Their clothes and their night both ruined simultaneously. Their feelings must be vented and avenged.

The chase was on. Mickey and Georgie fled up Chamber to Rose Street, a dark winding street that led to City Hall where they could hide in the park. Paulie, who was the fastest human I knew, decided to go down Hague Street and make a left on Oak and then down to Roosevelt Street seeking refuge at the Fulton Fish Market. I followed. It was definitely a run for your life. Paulie had a great advantage, but my fate was a lot more certain. I had the endurance, but was slow afoot. Our first encumbrance was a motion picture being made on Roosevelt Street. There were bright lights and I believe they were actually shooting the film before Paul and I intruded on their set like two blurs. I believe the picture was *Double Life* with Ronald Coleman.

The *big guys* now had a posse and were in full pursuit. Our hearts were beating furiously as we raced down South Street. Paul thought it would be better if we headed to Battery Park, but cut through Wall Street. Remember, in the 1940s no one worked downtown after 6:00 p.m. The downtown area was a complete ghost town where only cats and rats were to be seen. It was very quiet, which gave us an advantage. We ran all the way down to Battery Park and took our first break. I was exhausted, but felt good, and Paulie was in terrific shape. Our goal was to catch up to Georgie and Mickey at City Hall. We decided to go north on Broadway, meet with them, and try to sneak back to our homes.

On Broadway and Fulton we heard the banging of bats and chains and could distinguish the voices of the *big guys*. We saw them, and they saw us. Paulie and I ran down John Street cut over to Hague Street where there were trucks parked overnight and thought perhaps we could hide in those trucks. We did hide there, not knowing the *big guys* knew all about these trucks...they hung out in and around them. We got in, we slumped down in the cab but the mob was now here and like sniffing bloodhounds, they opened the cab doors one by one in each truck. They opened my side and I saw Charlie Lang's eyes. Paulie saw Joe Lapi. It was over. Our passion was to begin.

We were tied up and brought down to St. James Place to a rag shop owned by V. Ponte and Sons where there was a loading platform. There they placed Paul and me and later Georgie and Mickey; they got caught as well. They released the chains on our wrists and laid us out crucifix style, legs straight. Bobby C. and Roger Monk inflicted the first blows, tremendous blows to the biceps and thighs. Our legs and arms were now humming with pain and numbness. Then they rolled up our shirts and continued to inflict damage to our bodies. First Charlie Lang then Freddy Baloney, then Bopo, and Bimbo...each slapping our stomachs in a steady motion, pounding with an open hand. The torture continued as we began falling into oblivion, our eyes rolling and our bodies in seething pain. As I lay on that concrete platform I wondered what I would look like if I survived. As the last smack hit my stomach I lay there motionless, completely without feeling. I turned and saw Paulie moaning along with Mickey and Georgie. Our stomachs turned crimson and you could see each vein.

But oh! What do we tell our parents when we arrive home? Pain and suffering we must accept, for surely the happiness in seeing those eggs hit their mark was the happiness that kept us going. We had established ourselves and perhaps the *big guys* would relent from taunting us. Perhaps...perhaps.

Chapter Twenty

The pain continued to linger after our disastrous attempt to punish the *big guys*. The black and blue marks remained to show on our bodies. The summer continued in choking heat and our athletic abilities were diminished because of the physical assault on our limbs. This curtailed our recreational sports activities, considering it took three weeks for me to raise my right arm no less look at my stomach and see every vein that crossed the outer layer of my repository for food and drink. This was the first time we had to retreat from sports. What was thought to be a huge victory over the *big guys* now seemed a myth with dead arms and legs and no appetite to soothe my bellyache. Could it be that the *big guys* were really the winners???

Nahhhhhhhh!

The summer days were extremely hot on the Lower East Side with rooftop tar melting and streets exuding steam from the pavement. Relief from the elements was difficult. No air conditioning or large fans, no cross ventilation, no environmental laws on the books either. This was the weather and it was up to you to find a solution.

A solution was indeed found! Two short blocks east on Roosevelt Street was the East River and right above Roosevelt Street at this point was the Brooklyn Bridge, with a Department of Sanitation garbage collection barge ready to receive refuse twenty-four hours a day. Georgie, Mickey and I went to this watering hole one day because the heat had been unbearable. Lo and behold, many of the *big guys* were also there, but their intentions were to dive into the river, sans clothes, with the specific purpose of getting as cool as possible. Paulie, for some reason, was absent that day and we missed him because he always provided a vitality to all of us, and heaven knew we needed it. As we approached the pier we saw this old Italian man facing the Brooklyn side sitting on a folding chair with a line in the water and jingle bells attached to it. What was this? We were never exposed to outdoor sports like fishing and hunting. This elderly man was attempting to catch eels. As soon as the big guys noticed us they knew right away that they had to take action.

Let's reflect for a moment and see how a Lower East Side kid thinks. We had just come off this major battle for the corner of Roosevelt and St. James Place and now both sides were wary of each other, and it was natural for the big guys to take the initiative. They immediately sniffed us out because their clothes were piled upon the pier and we had a good shot of taking them while they were in the water. But they were smarter and even more aggressive. They pulled off all our clothes, including our underwear, and threw us in.

This was to be my first swimming lesson. I struggled to keep afloat only to be dunked by Charlie Lang and Richie Igor. Freddie Baloney happened to be there and he relished the attempted drownings. This was horrifying, but for some reason I wasn't afraid. After the dunkings, the big guys attempted to teach us to swim. They were refreshed by the cool water and their temperaments improved. We were scared shitless. Here we were, three young kids under the age of fifteen, mortified by our public nudity and intimidated in a sea of water filled with big guys, condoms, eels, debris, garbage, oil, and literally floating shit all around us. But...what a way to cool off!

Chapter Twenty-one

The summer was over and the chill of winter was upon us with a vengeance. It was around the holidays that we saw snow and bitter cold winds. Our remedy to offset the elements was an intense interest in sports. All of us would follow professional and college football, especially good team rivals. We had the football Giants and Yankees, the great Cleveland Browns team and Green Bay vs. Lions rivalries. Georgie and I absolutely admired one player in particular, a non New York Giant. His name was Tobin Rote, a quarterback who could throw seventy yards on the run. We were mesmerized by his throwing arm. Of course to keep warm, we went to the Sixty-ninth Regiment Armory on Saturday nights to watch the Knicks with Harry Gallitin, Sweetwater Clifton, and Sid Tanenbaum. On Sunday it would be the Rovers and the Rangers at the Garden. It was great to be a Manhattan kid, because everything was close by subway or bus. However, these joyous events were expensive. We needed the high school discounts to help us get in.

The avoidance of winter conditions meant that improvisation was necessary. Paul, Mickey, Georgie, and I took it upon ourselves, as did some of the big guys, to construct a wooden shack on Hague Street. This area was uninhabitable and desolate at night. We picked up a lot of loose wood, bought some nails, and put up the shack. Inside, we made a fire on the concrete and lit up our loose cigarettes (loosies) purchased at Stingy's on Oak Street. Our clothes were permeated with smoke and soot from this irreverent fire. On one occasion my mother smelled my breath and caught a whiff of cigarette odor. That spelled the end of my cigarette smoking, as I was the obedient son.

At other times, we found refuge and warmth at the public gym on Cherry Street. This edifice contained public baths and recreational activities. Our main purpose was the basketball court where we encountered a variety of neighborhood guys. They were somewhat older and more aggressive, with a lot more bullying. Anthony V., Beansie, Chili, Ray S., and Lou Fox. We also met other kids from the neighborhood, namely from Madison and James streets such as the McCaffrey brothers and a boy named Rudy Riska.

Beansie and Chili were terrific basketball players, but a skinny kid named Rudy was my choice in a game. In fact, he evolved as the best athlete ever in our neighborhood. This tall gangly rosy-cheeked boy lived on Madison Street with his brother Steve who was also a very good athlete. Their parents, Rudy and Betty, were of Czechoslovakian decent and gave every ounce of their love to these boys; as the boys became men, they gave it back. Rudy could take a ball to the hoop better than anybody in the neighborhood.

The games were intense, but what made basketball different was that those who liked to play were very good. In fact, of those who played, all or most were very good; hence, the intensity of the competition. On a cold, clear night, Georgie and I put on our sneakers and went to the gym. On a choose up, three on three, Georgie, Rudy, and I were linked up to play Ray S., Lou Fox, and Mickey McCaffrey. This was a good, even match. As the game went on it was getting very physical. Something had to give here. Then it happened; Georgie was getting roughed up and exploded. He grabbed Lou Fox, pushed him into the wall, and began pummeling him with lefts and rights to the body. Lou started to slump down as his back leaned against the wall. Georgie made a huge mistake by backing off. Lou recovered quickly and began to throw punches at Georgie...left, right, left, right...and Georgie went down. Rudy and I dragged Georgie behind the handball court to revive him.

It was always the case growing up that no one backed down. I don't care if somebody wrestled you on the street for fun or you got into an altercation at a game. Any challenge was met with a winner and a loser. As a matter of fact, every day from the ages of about eight–sixteen somebody would always challenge me to physical contact. This trait actually initiated and embedded in me a sense of joy in this physical contact because as you got bigger and those occasions grew more repetitive you naturally got better at it. What is an enigma here, is the fact that most of us did not like or want confrontation and had character traits of kindness and softness, but when that first slap hit your face or you were punched in the stomach, your temperament took on incredible energy and anger. After all, peer pressure was profound given the heavy population of kids and teenagers on any given block. If you wanted to survive and enjoy the activities you could not back off. You had no choice and you were mandated to be a survivor.

We often laugh now at how many individuals in the media boast of their toughness in the other borough neighborhoods where they grew up. "This was the toughest neighborhood" or "That was the toughest neighborhood." What bullshit! Those outer borough neighborhoods were sanctuaries for those who left our neighborhood. Sure you had rough kids, but we were the best at it. Like any sport, if you practice every day you were the best. The most accurate testimony as to why anyone would live on the Lower East Side would be to say you were there because of a birth, a plane, or a boat. No one came from another borough or another city or state. Everyone in our neighborhood climbed out...no one climbed in.

Chapter Twenty-two

As the holidays approached and the weather turned colder we concentrated on football and basketball. There were many football games—Army/Navy, Notre Dame/USC, Auburn and all the top schools. Our interest was who would be the best players in the pros. On Sunday it would be the Giants. Every football star was imitated in the neighborhood. A leather football was a rare item in those days. Usually one of the big guys had one and it was always over-inflated, which meant a bullet from the passer would crush your chest. More often than not, Paulie, Georgie, and I had to make our footballs out of the *Daily News* folded and wrapped with a cord. Our baseballs were taped white because the cover was off and the softball clinchers were always marked up to $2.50 by Johnny Mazza who controlled Park Street. Pink

Spauldeens were always stolen from Herman's World of Sporting Goods on Nassau Street. They were fifteen cents if purchased.

The most eventful winter was the snowstorm of 1947. Madison Street literally had a two-story mountain of snow on its sidewalks. Snow was sticking to the streets and traffic was nil. We had the whole street to ourselves. I remember one kid who was nicknamed Lorke, after a Giant ballplayer named Lucky Lorke. On this particular day of the storm, he brought out a sled. Indeed, this was a huge treat for all of us. I always wanted to *belly wop* and go as far as I could. Nobody could afford a sled, much less keep it in the apartment.

Lorke and I decided to perform a double belly wop, which meant he went first and then I would jump on top of him. The snow was still falling and as we headed south, and a huge oil truck was heading toward us. Visibility was poor due to snow. All I could remember is that I looked up after I jumped on to see this fuel truck already upon us. Lorke had the steering arms in his hands but froze and I could not decide fast enough whether to jump off or not. It was too late. The driver never saw us. We went under the truck. Were it not for the high clearance of the fuel truck I would not be writing of this event. We cleared it, or should

I say, I cleared the undercarriage and came out at the other end.

It was so sudden and the fright so brief it quickly became exhilaration after we passed through. I went home that night and looked out at the Third Avenue El and watched the sparks fly on the third rail. This was all part of a very magic winter.

Chapter Twenty-three

The winters were certainly brutal and Paulie and I were now becoming very close. We enjoyed our rendezvous with the belly treatments and with the snow on the ground and on the roofs. We had a great time pelting the big guys. After all, we had no sleds, skates, or snowboards. Confrontation was our outlet. As the gray skies of winter started to show, we found refuge in two places of interesting entertainment. One was the Venice Theatre. This palace of western serials, cartoons, and movies was considered a bug house due to its proximity to the Bowery. It was not considered particularly clean, but like all the other theatres, it had a balcony, mainly for the smokers. It was owned by a woman called Mazie. She was a Jewish woman who was rumored to be the heiress of valuable properties. This was never verified, but nonetheless she was perhaps the most generous human being in our neighborhood. Mazie was up in age and always had a ton of makeup on and wore high heels with a leopard skin coat. When you attended the Venice Theatre you would pay the cashier a dime or fifteen cents to see a full program of cartoons, western serials, newsreels, and a double feature. Mazie would be next to the cashier's booth handing out joke books and comics and many a time we didn't have enough money for admission. Mazie would let us in time and time again. Because the Bowery was so close to the Venice Theatre, there was an abundance of derelicts and alcoholics. Mazie always gave them money. She also gave significant amounts to the Catholic churches although she was of the Jewish faith. Everyone loved Mazie. She always said hello to the kids on her way home. In a way she was the Mother Teresa of the neighborhood.

The Venice Theatre always showed the best western serials and movies. Everybody in the neighborhood loved cowboy movies. They piqued our imaginations. The West was fascinating to urban kids. We had the best: the Durango Kid, Hopalong Cassidy, Lash La Rue, Zorro, Roy Rogers, the Lone Ranger, and tons of other cowboys. The Venice Theatre captured our imaginations because the news serials showed current highlights of the war, national news, and sports. This segment was always an attraction because it showed highlights of the Army/Navy games, Notre Dame, and the other big schools, featuring running by Doc Blanchard and Glenn Davis and passing by Johnny Lujack. The movies were always great because of Humphrey Bogart, James Cagney, Edward G. Robinson, and Spencer Tracy. Double features all the time.

Many of us would bring our lunch because we could not afford to buy any food. Many times there would be disruptions in the theater. These outbursts would be handled by the chief usher, *Duck Feet*...a descriptive way of characterizing how this man walked. However, it is said that he once was tossed over the balcony and he never returned.

The Tribune, on the other hand, was a classier theatre only steps from City Hall. Here you had a cozier venue with features like *Tammy* and *Sayonara* and *On The Waterfront*. While this theatre was less raucous than the Venice, we managed to play a few tricks here as well. One Sunday, the busiest day for the movies, Mickey, Paul, and I went over to City Hall Park to feed the pigeons with the idea that we would catch one and release it at the appropriate time in the theatre. During the playing of the main feature we released the pigeon, which flew around inside unharmed and free but when the projector light caught the bird it shadowed across the screen one hundred times it size. It looked like *Rodan.* The place was packed and panic and bedlam ensued as the theatre emptied and the police arrived to investigate this sighting of a monster. We left very calmly and went to the cashier to seek a refund. Another pleasant and amusing Sunday, to say the least.

Chapter Twenty-four

If the cruel winters allowed, we would get a warm sunny day when we would retreat to *the lots*, a parcel of land directly under the Manhattan Bridge. It was filled with debris, and even contained blood from derelicts and homeless men from the Bowery who tragically jumped off the bridge to end lives of despair and anguish. In warm weather it served the neighborhood as the official hardball field and in winter, as a two-hand touch football field. My very first experience at this *facility* was as a young kid watching the big guys play on a Saturday morning. Someone hit a foul ball, straight up, the catcher looked up, got in position, threw away his glove, kept his mask on and caught the ball. This could happen only on the Lower East Side.

What a place these lots were for us. Despite all the adversarial elements, we enjoyed our games, whether with a taped up baseball or a wrapped, stitched football. We hit the crap out of the ball and threw seventy-yard passes. We all dreamed and relished our sports accomplishments even though at times we had to make big sacrifices, such as when a baseball went over the wall...our only ball! I climbed up the fence and as I tried to finesse my way over the barbed wire, my hand got caught, right below the pinky and into the meaty part of my hand. I hung there for a full half hour before I could get someone to help me. I felt crucified and lost every morsel of energy in me. Thank God Joe L got my hand free. This harrowing moment and the condition that prevailed left a bitter taste in my mouth for our *city fathers*. When I pass through the neighborhood today I see a miniature stadium with lights adjacent to the lots. To this day, the inactions of those politicians are unforgivable.

It was now 1954 and the low-income housing projects were completed. The neighborhood started to change. We now had blacks and Puerto Ricans living in these projects mixed with some of the displaced citizens as well as the Chinese moving in from Chinatown. The transition was not necessarily an easy one. These projects were still surrounded by the same Fourth Ward residents. Initially there were confrontations. The remaining citizens of our neighborhood were incompatible with the newly arrived groups. The question was why? The reason for this question was more profound in our neighborhood. Was it race? I and many others felt it was not skin color or different physical attributes or language. How could it be? We loved Jackie Robinson, Roy Campanella, and my all-time favorite, Willie Mays. Maybe it was a race issue in baseball with all the southern players. Not here on the Lower East Side. This was the bastion of tolerance. Only by the grace of God was our skin color it was. Our neighborhood was and probably still is today the most diverse section of the city, or for that matter, the United States. We all got along extremely well. Irish, Italians, Jews, Greeks, Spanish, Slovaks, Poles, and Asians. This, after generations of assimilation starting after the Civil War. The difference here was culture. When you have no commonality in subjects of culture there is resistance to integration, whether it is music, language, dress, morals, food, or lifestyle. The only road to integration and acceptance is the Americanization of oneself. This process has been repeated over and over again since the birth or our nation. Let us hope and pray that it will continue.

Chapter Twenty-five

Roosevelt Street, all two hundred yards of it that remained, started to change. Some people were starting to move out as rumors circulated of destroying Roosevelt Street and its beloved Church, St. Joachim, to make room for a modern housing cooperative. The Korean War ended and many of the older guys were returning from the armed services and had begun to settle down. Everyone now seemed to consider a vocation in life. One kid entered the seminary, another started a doo-wop singing group that is still successful today, and others started to focus on education and better jobs.

As teenagers, we still had a lot of oats left in us and while Roosevelt Street was transforming itself, we were just beginning our journeys into manhood. After all, our moment of maturation had arrived already in our

earlier years. By fourteen, most of us were hung by our
ankles and held into the sewers to retrieve Spauldeens.
Some were even held over rooftops by their ankles as
fun. We climbed over barbed wire fences. Paulie and
Joe L. humped their way—back and feet—in a narrow
alleyway up four stories. We swam in the currents of
the East River and jumped on rooftops—building to
building. Basic training came early for all of us. We
did not need to be soldiers, sailors, cops, fireman, or
longshoremen to become men. As someone once said,
"When you are born in this neighborhood, you are born
with a pair of balls!"

The population our age was now sparse, so kids
on our portion of Roosevelt Street migrated to the
other streets. Some went to St. James Street, some to
Baxter Street. Paulie, Mickey, and I chose to hang
out on William Street. Georgie had already moved
to Brooklyn and taken up golf and fishing. Golf and
fishing? Unheard of in our neighborhood. These were
sissy sports. We could not believe that Georgie had lost
his mind. He was indeed ahead of his time.

William Street was an appealing block physically. It
was a short section of a longer William Street that ran
all the way past Wall Street. This was the only section
that had residential apartments and a smattering of
commercial activities. This section of William Street ran

approximately one hundred yards between Chambers Street and Pearl Street. When Paulie, Mickey, and I arrived, there were already a few guys and girls living and hanging out here. Eugene B., Bobby T., Johnny B., Ray B., Willie and Eddy P., Fat Marty, Nonnie, Dom, Augie, and a few others. The girls were very pretty on this block. Marie, Emily, Carolyn, Tootsie, Joyce, and Ann Marie. For some reason, other guys and girls were attracted to here. We had many from nearby Baxter Street. Johnny M. and Joe F.

It was interesting to observe the different activities that took place. You had a famous bar and grill, *Augrick's*, which had the only *stainless steel* bar top in New York City at the time. Gathered here on a daily basis was a confluence of characters consisting of politicians, bookmakers, detectives, and a few locals. Next to the bar was a firehouse, Engine 12, where we basically hung out with the firemen who made us our stickball bats.

Paulie and I were still going to high school and as we integrated smoothly with one another; things were changing. The bar was sold after two generations of family ownership. A woman bought it and we promptly called her *Broadway Rose*. She opened a miniature hall above her, which she used for special occasions and as a sleeping facility when working and hung over from 4:00 a.m. the night before. The new ownership brought new customers. Now we were seeing people from Monroe Street, Madison Street, James Street, and even North of Canal Street. Some guys we knew, the others we didn't. As the months went by, most of us had reached drinking age. None of us really drank in excess, but enjoyed a couple of beers after playing a game. At night, after a money stoopball game, Paulie, Mickey, and I enjoyed a Tom Collins in a good sized plastic container and hung out on the corner.

As the weeks went by, it seemed more and more guys were hanging out on William Street; one by one, an immigration wave had begun to take shape. This small section off William Street was now a hub for people coming from James Street, the Projects, Upper Madison Street, Baxter Street, and sometimes all the way down on Albany Street. Girls that some of the guys met at a dance were invited down. Most were from New Jersey. These girls had cars...we didn't.

Suddenly, this little street transformed itself into a mini Main Street. As time went by, someone opened up a diner called the Ranch. It was a bacon and eggs joint. The owner, Joe, was a gambler. He loved to play cards. By circumstance there was an empty store on the block used by a semi-retired import/export individual, John Mearns. This individual loved his drink and his cards. He set up a card table in his store, where Joe

Ranch, Peter the old Greek, John Mearn himself, and a few of the other *old reliables* engaged in a good card game. However, one day when things got tight, Joe Ranch—apparently having a funding crisis—abruptly got up from his chair and ran back to his diner. No one knew what happened. After a few minutes he returned struggling with the huge cash register from his restaurant and the game promptly resumed. Joe needed substantial funding and he made sure it was literally available. After these games were concluded, John M. was inebriated and, as usual, had to be assisted to his apartment. He went willingly, but always required assistance. He usually asked a couple of us to escort him, but he clamped on his enablers, squeezing their arms with his, and we found it difficult to release ourselves from his vice-like grip. Only after we laid him in bed did he release these devastating clamps.

Activity on the block varied from stickball to stoopball to card games, with Paulie G. sweeping up the change with his bluffs and luck. Every sport had bets attached. The most ferocious betting took place on the stoopball games where we would play with six-man teams, each player betting $2. Stoopball was always played around the corner on Pearl Street.

Chapter Twenty-six

Pearl Street intersected William Street and at the same time was the only street to intersect Broadway twice. Here we played stoopball and two-hand touch because it was a wide street. We had markers like the entrance to 441 Pearl—hitting this was an automatic home run. Every game had bets on it. Outside guys would bet as well as the players. I hated to bet, but it made the game more fun. Since the eighth grade at St. James School I had given up betting. There, however, I took bets with my classmate Frankie C. We went partners and took bets on baseball. The odds were 8 to 1. You picked three major league players to get six hits combined in a day. The bet limit was .10 cents. We were doing great until one day there was heavy betting on Williams, Musial, and Kenny Keltner of the Indians.

They collected ten hits among them and it broke our bank. We had to borrow to pay off. Finis!

On the street we met a newcomer called Pete. He came from Knickerbocker Village and his parents owned a butcher shop in the West Village. His physical makeup was very distinct from the other human beings. His body conformed to that of an ape. His head was big and square, he had very wide shoulders, a twenty-inch neck, and a size twenty-nine waist. His biceps and arms resembled a side of beef. His introduction to William Street was conspicuous since he owned a 1949 Cadillac—this was the only car owned by someone in the neighborhood. William Street had now taken on a life of its own, becoming a mini melting pot in the neighborhood, a quasi refugee camp where it seems everyone from the neighborhood congregated.

A natural assimilation took place with guys and girls from Baxter Street, James Street, Roosevelt Street, Madison Street, Mulberry Street, the Projects, and Monroe Street; all now utilizing William Street as headquarters. Because the population was growing, we branched out to Pearl Street, north and south. Here we enjoyed our sports with great joy, whether it was two-hand touch, football, or stickball. The bets always increased the intensity and ferocity of each game. Tempers often flared and oftentimes punches were thrown. I remember on one occasion when our stoop was blocked by a Volkswagen Beetle. This car had to be moved. The doors were locked. Not to worry. Pete the Lash, with his superhuman strength, back to the rear bumper, lifted the car. With the rear wheels off the ground he moved it forward. We had never witnessed anything near this human superstrength. None of us ever saw Pete lift a weight in exercise. This kid was thick, a strong ape disguised as a human being. I liked Pete; he made us all laugh a lot. His nickname, Pete the Lash, was concocted after the West Point running back Pete Lash. Later on, however, some of us would experience his strength. Woe is me!

On a very memorable occasion, I recall a choose-up game with many of the guys from William Street participating. It was a very hot night and we all bet on the game. As usual, it was a close game. Then it happened—a throw home, a hard slide, a tag. Out or safe? Each team called its own play. No umpires. Paulie G. and I were on the same team. Pete the Lash on the other team. As fate would have it, Paulie was coming home and Pete was waiting for the throw from the outfield. The Spaldeen was whipped in, Paulie slid on the diamond plate in front of the stoop and then Pete made a hard tag to the jaw of Paulie G. The volcano erupted with Paulie springing to his feet, swinging a right hand to Pete the Lash's head. Everyone swarmed home plate. Pete immediately put a vice-like clamp on Paulie's head as Paulie G. flailed his fists at Pete's balls and chest while moving closer to the street. Hitting Pete was like hitting a steel girder. Nonetheless, Paulie G. was afraid of no man; a son of Italy, he was nine when Nazis threatened his mother, brothers, and sisters as a multitude of German soldiers occupied their home during World War II.

The two rolled around in the gutter until cooler heads prevailed. I tried to break up the fight but unbeknownst to me the others were brawling. Everything now became intertwined as I attempted to break the lock on Paulie G.'s neck as it was being crushed. I felt a sharp blow to the top of my head. Down I went, flattened out on the street. This, the very same type of street that would often be the repository of my body for ten years. Most every day I would have an altercation with someone. My sturdy frame was attuned to this type of violence, made only more aggressive with the use of my hands in self-defense. This time, however, someone really lowered a hammer. As I got to my feet and saw Paulie and Pete separated, and everyone cooled off, I noticed that I was bleeding from my head. In those days, we did not go to the hospital. We poured water over the wound and hoped it would dry up by the time we got home, and that it did.

All these games introduced an aggressiveness that resembled male dominance in a jungle. This behavior, though never invited, was absolutely required to survive and provided a level of enjoyment. Hard to believe.

Chapter Twenty-seven

Our neighborhood, while smaller geographically than one could imagine, had a certain fragrance and ambiance to it. The winter drove us in and made us explore other venues, while summer pushed us out as long and as late as the body could tolerate. At times this caused a certain restlessness. We felt compelled to seek adventure. The usual suspects were Times Square, Greenwich Village, the Jazz Hall on Sixth Street, or the St. George Hotel—this our only visitation right to Brooklyn, other than Coney Island.

One Friday evening there were many of us gathered on the corner of William and Pearl streets. Pete the Lash pulled up in his 1949 green Cadillac and the boys became itchy. Where to go? There were about eight of us and we decided to go to the St. George Hotel. The decision was to meet at eight and go over the Brooklyn Bridge and go for a swim. Maybe we would get lucky and meet some girls.

We swam and had a lot of fun, although we did not see any girls, but there was an abundance of fairies, as we called them then. These were the same creatures who admired our endowments and attributes in the shower and sauna areas. As we exhausted all our athletic abilities, we retreated from the gym and pool and proceeded to the showers. The showers were all open stalls and with eight guys ball-assed naked, there was bound to be trouble. It began with towel whipping, soap throwing, splashing, pushing, shoving, and all the excitement that went with it. In my case, I was showering next to Pete the Lash. It seemed unavoidable. Pete initiated the action with spraying the water and then using his towel to redden my ass. I retaliated by smacking him with a quick left jab. That was it. This classic began with water running and each us delivering crushing blows to the body. Here was a young man weighing 215 at five feet nine, with the torso of an ape and a body of steel, fighting a developing nineteen-year-old male, six feet one, 185 pounds, with a quickness of hands. The remaining spectators, some without male hormones, retreated, while our guys watched in awe as Pete and I delivered bone-crunching blows to each other's naked bodies . . . vital organs swinging in the air. First a vicious blow to my left chest and then a thunderous right to Pete's stomach, each delivering wicked blows to the chest, ribs, and stomach with cascades of water drenching our bodies, which were turning black and blue after a full five minutes of intense contact. We finally stopped after shear exhaustion. Our bodies stood up well, but in the days that followed, their frailties became painfully evident.

It was brutal and tough indeed but gratifying in a very strange way. I always enjoyed contact and Pete did too. There was a certain exhilaration to all of this, perhaps strange and irrational, but it manifested itself in our daily desires for competitiveness and superiority. I was determined to beat this ape, the strongest human in the neighborhood.

Chapter Twenty-eight

As summer was coming to a close, things were starting to change. I heard from Rudy R., playing then in Triple A ball for the Yankee organization. He had developed bursitis in his pitching arm. It turned out that this ended his career in professional baseball. The neighborhood was rooting for Rudy. He was our favorite son and had recently been invited to Yankee spring training by manager Casey Stengel. Rudy was an athletic icon. He could toss a basketball through the hoop almost at will and do everything splendidly in baseball. A great receiver in football and then later in life, he excelled in tennis, golf, and handball.

Things were getting itchy now. We all needed to compete in different ways. The nights were very hot and windless. The crowd from outside William Street was growing and we started to get a little closer to each other. On a very steamy night, however, an incredible sea change took place. It seemed everyone congregated at William and Pearl Streets that night. A soft rain had begun to fall and, of course, there were some who cherished their hairstyles, such as Paulie and Richie the Comb. We all sought shelter at 441 Pearl Street. This was a twelve-story commercial building utilized by us as a stoopball marker; its entrance indicated the perimeter of right field in our stoopball games. Tonight, however, it would house what would always be known as the neighborhood's *fight of the century*.

Inside the vestibule of 441 Pearl Street there were a dozen or so guys seeking shelter from the elements. As time passed, the natural testosterone display took shape. Pete the Lash threw a couple of left-hand smacks to my head. I did not immediately retaliate, but instead said if we had some boxing gloves we could go at it. Someone mentioned he had a pair and would go get them. These *dogs* were waiting and hoping for a good fight between Pete and me, as they required some entertainment for that night.

Down deep I really wanted this brawl. Pete was an excellent target with his wide shoulders and square head. Given his bully practices and superior physical strength, I needed to satisfy myself that I could beat this guy. It was a tough choice, however, since the consequences could be dire for me. One good crack from Pete's fist could break my jaw and render me unconscious. Not to worry! My mind was made up to beat the shit out of him, despite the fact that I had been a recipient of his brutal strength in the showers not too long ago.

One of the guys brought the gloves. They were about eight ounces. The tension started to build as everyone was now exuding tremendous anticipation. The de facto ring would be as follows: the floor was constructed of mosaic tile, on one side a steel banister, on the other a marble wall. The other sides completed the ring. The main entrance of double glass doors was opposite a steel elevator door. These components were a blueprint for mortal combat.

We put on our gloves and bobbed a little on the tile floor. This was to be a three-round bout with three minutes per round. A referee was selected and the timekeeper would be one guy, the only guy with a watch. A stick was used to strike the steel banister for round one.

We circled each other looking out for any offensive that would begin. I was always better if I got the first hit. The adrenalin would surge and I would become a better fighter because my hand speed would increase, notwithstanding my temper, which would begin to boil. Pete threw the first punch, a flailing right hand that missed my head. He followed with a charging left hook that caught me on the side of my head. This was now the catalyst. I became very angry once I was hit. I circled Pete counterclockwise and jabbed him in that square face enough to see it redden. I slammed him with a left hook and right to the side of the head. His eyes began to swell. I jabbed and jabbed until round one was over. Pete began a new strategy. He had to overcome my reach, so he began to charge in throwing roundhouse lefts and rights, trying to smash me down. He caught me with a right to the mouth, cutting my lip, which began to bleed. We exchanged a good flurry of rights and lefts as we had in a previous fight at the Hotel St. George. At this point, the fight was even. I won round one, Pete round two. The last round exhausted us both as we tried to put out the other's lights throwing wild lefts and rights, often ending up in a clinch. When you clinched Pete you were subject to punishment rather than a respite from the punches. His large head would nestle under your chin and if there was any movement to free it, you would jeopardize your teeth as one upward movement of his head would be the equivalent of a sledgehammer hitting its target. Round three ended and we both staggered to the steps exhausted from all the blows thrown and received. Given the intensity and brutality of the fight, we both came out of it in good shape—I with a swollen lip and Pete with a swollen black eye.

The debate on who had won the fight continued for a few days with Paulie G. pronouncing me the winner based on his complete and total partiality. This was some fight. No one before except Paulie G. had challenged Pete and his enormous physical strength. I came away feeling good but disappointed that I should have done better. On the other hand I could have received a terrible beating as well as a split head off the marble wall. What a way to get some entertainment!

Chapter Twenty-Nine

After the *fight of the century,* school was over, summer was in and everyone was out. As William Street proliferated into a mini-village, a certain anxiety and restlessness prevailed. Everyone worked during the day to support themselves and their families. Those few of us who attended college paid our own tuition and none of us dared ask our parents for help. As in most neighborhoods at that time, sports overshadowed all other interests simply because our generation had few options for entertainment. Distractions were few and money scarce. The result meant happiness within the confines of our neighborhood. The only real venue for entertainment without excessive cost was participation in sports. This could be exemplified in sports in the street, mainly stickball, stoopball, punchball, or softball, or, if there was a field available, hardball. The other sports that drew considerable interest were basketball and football. Those of us who played basketball were influenced by the New York Knicks and the bitter city winters. This forced us into available gyms to keep warm and active and thus, basketball.

Football was always attractive to the guys in our neighborhood. We played it many different ways—on the streets with a rolled-up *Daily News* tied with twine or perhaps a two-hand touch game in the streets, sewer to sewer. The most enjoyable, however, was playing tackle in City Hall Park or in the park in front of Foley Square...sans equipment. The game always fascinated me because of its head-to-head contact and because my father exposed me to the game at a very early age. He took me up to the Polo Grounds where two thousand people would show up to witness professional football. It would be freezing and Dad would cover me with a horse blanket that weighed more than I did. These fresh memories of Don Hudson and Ken Strong always tantalized my mind. I always wanted to be them.

Paulie and I had a brilliant conversation one day in early summer. *Why don't we organize a football team?* We looked over the population of William Street, James Street, and the Smith Projects and concluded that there were enough of us who loved the game and had played it before. Most of us at the time were in our late teens or early twenties, but a few were in their midtwenties. After an informal survey of who would be interested, it appeared that more than thirty of us would play. The desire to play was never an issue. Ironically, none or very few had played football in high school. But all of us were raised in the streets where guts, heart, and courage had grown within us. Lack of fear would overcome lack of talent. After all, this was a physical game, albeit good strategy. It was a predictable mix of short, tall, fat, skinny, slow, and fast.

Nonetheless, it represented more than a quorum and demonstrated the desire for all of us to unite with a good solid activity. We had to have a focal point, such as a place for meetings, organization, and planning. It was fortunate at this time that many of us attended St. Andrew's Church for Sunday Mass. Here many attendees were from William and Baxter streets, which were in close proximity to the church. More important, however, was the fact that there was a young priest assigned there who had a sincere interest in youthful activities. He had recently been assigned to St. Andrew's from Staten Island. As we all became introduced to Father Orson, he encouraged us to form a Holy Name Society. At ages nineteen or twenty, many of us had served as altar boys. This process had ensured our spiritual growth combined with our attending Catholic schools. Farther Orson took genuine and deep interest in the formation of our adult lives. He married many of us and said funeral masses for our parents. This was extraordinary since St. Andrew's Roman Catholic Church was not a parish. It was a church to serve municipal, government, and court employees at the Civic Center.

Father Orson was the most junior of four priests assigned to St. Andrew's. The pastor, an intelligent man, was assigned the additional duty of overlooking the entire nun and religious population of the archdiocese. He was ably assisted by a dynamic priest and orator, Rev. T. V. Snee. The assistant pastor was Father Renschler, a steady and holy man. Msgr. Nelson did not and would not tolerate excessive noise. The church, located in the shadows of the municipal building and the federal courthouse, was almost eerie at night since there was little population nearby. Hence, when Father Orson approached the monsignor about establishing a Holy Name Society and perhaps some other social activities, Msgr. Nelson's response was always with warnings of caution and a list of caveats. In other words, keep everything low profile.

Paul and I had a dilemma. How were we going to approach Father Orson with our idea of forming a football team? In addition, we had to pick someone to coach us. We decided that it would be preferable to pick a coach since that person would be older and would instill discipline among the team members. If we did this first, and then approached Father Orson, we would have a better chance of having a football team called *St. Andrew's.*

Paul and I started to think about the coach. Who in the neighborhood had the character and wherewithal to give his time to coach eighteen- to thirty-year-old men? The more important question was who had football experience? After some discussion, we approached Coach Johnny B. who had played high school football and was an all city quarterback. Coach B. was a known and respected neighborhood athlete. The question was would he accept our invitation to coach our team? Did he have the constitution, patience, discipline and time to handle thirty basically diverse and energized young men? The answer in the end was yes.

Paul and I were elated because we thought that with Coach B.'s talent and class, we could convince Father Orson to sponsor a St. Andrew's football team. Our mission was finally accomplished and we were all fitted for uniforms, an event that was a first on the Lower East Side. Uniforms were treated as luxury apparel.

Chapter Thirty

The heat of the season returned and a lot of us were working at summer jobs. As we enjoyed our spare time after work, we decided that instead of visiting the Jersey shore, we would head north to Pine Plains, New York, where Paul had cousins and Mickey also had blood relatives who emigrated from Piacenza. This was a farm maintained by a couple of families. They had cattle, chickens, pigs, goats, and hunting dogs. Many older Italian men from Roosevelt Street went to Pine Plains to hunt deer and woodchucks. The latter creatures made huge holes, causing the cattle to injure themselves. As a result, many from Roosevelt Street were invited up to lodge, eat, and hunt.

Our trip was arranged by Paul and Mickey and necessitated exact planning. Our transportation, of course, was Pete's Caddy. Given the characteristics of the individuals, it was necessary that seating in the car was done with precision. Pete was the driver and I sat next to him in the middle because I was the only other licensed driver in case Pete failed at the wheel. Paulie G., on the other hand, sat by the front window where the side view mirror reflected his structured hairdo with his comb ever ready to keep him perfectly coiffed. Mickey sat behind Pete with Georgie in the middle and Raymond near the window, but behind hanging clothes. We decided this arrangement at 3:00 a.m. on a Saturday. Pete for some ridiculous reason wore dark blue glasses while driving in the black of night. Georgie and Paul smoked their cigarettes. Mickey constantly pulled on the driver's seat asking questions and giving directions, annoying Pete to no end. Raymond looked tortured sitting in the back with all those clothes, and Georgie kept puffing away. When we arrived in Pine Plains at 5:30 a.m., we decided to play a stickball game, using the side of the barn. The sun began to rise and here we were, six city kids playing a stickball game on a farm. We prepared for these events and even had a football in the trunk. After the game we visited the cousin who ran the boarding house and she had a complete breakfast waiting for us.

As we ate our breakfast, we contemplated our day. Who wanted to hunt, who wanted to go to the lake and see some girls, and who wanted to just hang around? Alas! We decided to go to the lake, where they had canoes and diving boards. There were a lot of kids there with the counselors, many our age. We participated in all the activities as the sun began burning us up. By 4:00 p.m. I'd had enough. I was severely burned and needed to go back to the lodge.

We left to return for dinner, but I was not up to it. I remained in bed suffering from the burn and in need of help. The other boys decided they were going to raid the counselor's camp that night. I was on the disabled list with a temperature and chills. I asked Mickey for an aspirin and he found one and brought to me without water. As he returned with the water he tripped and spilled the water on the aspirin, melting it. So much for my temporary cure. As I lay in bed suffering I felt dehydrated with burning pains and chills. My lips were parched. My friends no longer seemed interested, but instead were bent on raiding the camp. My exhaustion and pain took so much out of me that I fell asleep on my stomach. Around 3:00 a.m. I felt an ice cold liquid between the cheeks of my ass. I screamed as the cold beer penetrated my bedclothes. My friends showed compassion in strange ways.

By the next day I felt somewhat better and participated in some of the activities. I took a ride with

Mickey to go hunting, primarily for woodchucks. As we proceeded up a dirt road, we saw in front of us two red foxes, roughly sixty feet away. We stopped the car, pulled out our rifles and aimed at them directly from our car door windows. They stood motionless as we took aim. This would be easy. Pow! Pow! Shots echoed throughout the hills. The foxes ran away and we were stunned. There they were, standing before us—in full side view no less—and with the distance so short and our rifles so accurate, we missed both targets.

City kids once again proved their mettle as we both laughed at the incident. We were misfits, displaced for a weekend. While we were recounting our failures to the others, Pete the Lash decided that he was going to wrestle the bull that was on the farm. The bull was walking out of the barn and into the field when Pete decided he was going to twist the bull's neck to get him down. He grabbed the bull's horns and tried twisting his head. The bull resisted and dragged Pete with him some one hundred yards before Pete released his hands from the horns. This was another example of how clueless city kids could be about life on a farm.

Chapter Thirty-one

Summer was coming to an end and overlapping softball and football seasons were in motion. As preparation was being made for football, some very serious softball was being played during the summer. As I mentioned, we had uniforms for football. T-shirts were issued with our softball team's name on them. The name was Al Smith. The sponsor, a Democratic club in the neighborhood did not like the name. They preferred Alfred E. Smith, after the former governor and citizen of the Lower East Side. The softball games were intense, as a significant amount of side bets would take place. The players themselves would bet about $5 each. There were a good amount of windmill pitchers around the neighborhood, including Mimi Fats, Blondie, Johnny B., and a guy from the hook. On occasion we would play an outside team, mainly from Harlem, which included Lefty Long, a terrific windmill pitcher. We did not have a stopper but we were finally able to import one from New Jersey. His name was *Jimmy No-Eyes* because of his very light blue eyes. This kid could pitch windmill and had a rubber arm.

One of the most famous games we played was a rematch between Al Smith and the guys from the hook. They had beaten us in a twenty-one-inning game a few weeks before. These guys were tough as kids and remained that way through adulthood. You had the Kenny brothers, Bull and Pepsi, Kelly, Red Hastings, Joe Fallon, and Boopsie. This time we had a powerful addition to our team. Rudy Riska was the very best athlete to come out of our neighborhood and had just been released from the Yankee organization because of bursitis and damage to his pitching arm. We had our best on the field, Jimmy No-Eyes, Albino, Butch, Paulie, Anthony, Cookie, Rudy, Carlo, and me. The game took the form of the previous matchup, a tie until the tenth inning and Rudy delivered with a double to left center, scoring the winning run.

As football began to take shape, Coach B. became very involved and I knew that his level of interest was profound. He seemed to want to relive his own past in playing the game, making sure we executed to perfection.

He had a good cadre of coaches, two Angelos and an outsider named Label. Our team had a diverse range in ages from seventeen–thirty. Some of us were not fully mature. Our bodies varied from a five two quarterback to a six three end. The only true physical specimen who stood out was Pete the Lash. Now with shoulder pads and helmet, his silhouette was extraordinary.

We started the season with a win. I was moved from center to quarterback, but did not get the ball over the goal. Butch, our five two quarterback moved the team well. My claim to fame was my throwing arm, conditioned from a young age to throw long and hard. I was always more comfortable playing the center position where I could use my educated elbows.

Nonetheless, we went on into the season getting beaten up by every team. While excuses did not prevail with us, the truth be told, the other teams were all collections of high school and college players. It was enjoyable because every player who played enjoyed the game. We played each game to win, fought hard, and competed as nobody could. To be in an organized team environment with uniforms, coaches, and a playbook was nirvana to Lower East Side kids who had only dreams to live on. Our fantasies were being played out...win, lose, or draw.

Chapter Thirty-two

The football team was now attracting more people to William Street. In order to make sure our social life was not disintegrating, a few of the guys looked to get a social club underway. First they rented the top floor of an old commercial building on Park Row. It even had a kitchen. Here we conducted all of our social events, including card playing, betting on sports and horses, and shooting a game of pool.

On Saturday, however, it was showtime. Invite every girl you can with music, food, and drink, and every guy dreaming his fantasies. The girls came from all over, with the majority from William Street and James Street. There was, however, a group who came from New Jersey. Life seemed like a huge enigma. Here you had girls coming all the way from Kearney, New Jersey, in their cars to be with guys who had no cars, no money, and lived in old law tenements. They would climb five flights of stairs to dance close and maybe have a date in the future. The building they were entering was a scary, leaky, dark commercial edifice with a pawnshop on the ground floor. No elevator, but very creaky stairs...steps that led to teenage utopia. Where else could a nineteen-year-old male better fulfill his adventurous thoughts than by opening a door to a room filled with rock-and-roll music with good-looking girls warming your heart and removing your freezing ass from the cold outside.

To think, all the previous years as we watched the older guys on Saturday nights go out on dates as we huddled around lampposts and in doorways talking about girls only to be home at 10:00 p.m. with the late editions of the *News* and the *Mirror.* Our lives were leading us toward different forms of entertainment. If we did go out on a date, we usually tried to go to the Latin Quarter, the Metropole, or the Copacabana. Every dime we had we splurged to impress. Cabs to and fro. One of our assistant coaches was Bopo. He was a great guy who had a nice way of needling you. Paulie and I would always take the opportunity to pick up a postcard from one of these nightclubs and mail it to Bopo, signing... *The last of the good time Charlies!* These episodes would then transform into our being called the Gold Dust Twins...our behavior in earlier years was being transformed into that of social butterflies!

As the football team began to develop, we experienced what organizations can do for a group of young men who otherwise always acted or reacted on their own instincts. Coach B. was exposing us to training and discipline. Our record was a losing one over the few seasons that St. Andrew played, but we learned to play well together. None of us had ever played organized football. There were no leagues when we were smaller, no high school or college football. We were all street kids who had played tackle football without equipment on patches of grass and sometimes asphalt. Coach B. kept us together with the other coaches. We had chosen the right person to lead us.

Chapter Thirty-three

Upon completion of the football season, we entered the holiday season and began to really concentrate on girls. Everyone was in tip-top shape and most of us were in our late teens. The landlord of the building where our club was located notified us to move out. We were disappointed because the location was perfect with no residential neighbors to complain and O'Rourke's Bar, established in 1888, the only place of noise, fifty yards away. The club had become extremely important to us, as our social activities were heating up. Yes, we did have our St. Andrew's facility, but heaven forbid if a girl showed up in this sanctuary. Talk was always contained to Catholic behavior such as Mass, altar boy duty, acolytes, confession, and always the possibility of a vocational religious life. Father Orson had a resounding command of the conversation in a way similar to broadcast journalist Mike Wallace.

As our activities expanded, we concentrated on gathering in one or two places. This would be Augrick's Bar and Grill or the Pearl Tavern on Pearl Street. Augrick's, as previously mentioned, was no longer owned by the original family. It was now owned by a woman we named Broadway Rose. She was short, very plump, and on many occasions, due to circumstances, slept upstairs overnight. Because there we no shower facilities she would *freshen-up* by squirting heavy perfume under her arms and other vital areas...à la French trollop. One of her first actions upon acquiring the bar was to hire a barmaid. In this case, she hired an extremely attractive young woman, well packaged. Subsequently, this pleasant change attracted guys who had previously not been drawn to a bar near City Hall, federal and state courts, and the brass from the police department. A dramatic change was taking place in our own neighborhood and we could see the transformation. Most of the football team would often gather at the bar for drinks. But most of us did not drink much alcohol. We enjoyed mostly a cold beer in the summer. We would take out that large container of Tom Collins and share it after a stoopball game.

Because we had no facility to meet females, it was becoming difficult to arrange social events. Girls were very reluctant to go into a bar and grill at that time. It was not yet proper or accepted for those we referred to as *nice girls*. Some of us approached Broadway Rose and persuaded her to give up her temporary housing quarters upstairs and let us use it for our parties. We would buy our food and drink from her and she would let us use the upstairs. Rosie was a businesswoman, but had a soft spot for us. Many times she let us borrow her car to bring the Jersey girls home.

In between our social activities, we would go to dances on Twenty-third Street, Seventy-fifth Street, and to a jazz place on Sixth Street called the Central Plaza. This was a great place to meet chicks from all over the city. One hot night, however, we became involved in a huge riot at the Central Plaza. Near the end of the night, the famous musicians would play *When the Saints Go Marchin' In* and everyone would get up and march, one behind the other, to the music. On this occasion, we had about a dozen of us at our table. When the song began, everyone was getting up to march. Then, as I turned my head to see if the lads were following, I witnessed a chair flying in the air. The battle had begun, and there they were, all the boys of the neighborhood swinging it out. As I joined the fracas, we were on the offensive with the opposition against the wall. Glasses, chairs, and fists flailing away and blood flowing. The music stopped and security and the NYPD appeared. This was the first time that the music stopped when an altercation took place, but there were many to follow, since jazz and booze tend to soften the brain.

The brawl spilled out onto the street, but before that a lot had been going on. As a group we fared well against this Brooklyn group, pummeling them good! Don't ask me why or what happened or who was right or wrong. This was survival. The initial security contingent could not contain us, but when additional help came we were decimated. Doc and I were herded into an elevator and rubber hosed to a pulp. As we were thrown on our asses, we were met by the NYPD who booted us away as quickly as we got up. The brawl continued on the side streets where some were arrested. Doc and I walked home, hoping to reunite with the rest, which we did the next day in court. The judge dismissed the disorderly conduct charges, providing the arrested write a three-hundred-word composition on conduct...thanks to the pleas of our beloved priest and chaplain, Father Orson.

Chapter Thirty-four

Now that Broadway Rose acquiesced and allowed us to have our parties upstairs, we felt more upbeat. We could invite more girls and have bigger parties. As an alternative, we also went to the Pearl Tavern, which was owned by a guy named *Cheese*. Pete the Lash preferred the bar because the jukebox had the record *Night Train*. Pete would gyrate like a stripper and everyone would laugh like hell. He was better than a stripper. This bar attracted a different clientele. Noted well were the two occasions on which we were all congregated on the corner of Pearl and William streets when a car rolled by with the occupants firing bullets into the bar. The other memorable event happed on a July 4th evening when an unknown gentleman motioned some of us over to tell us to move away from the corner because he was going to explode a huge firecracker. We laughed but obliged the gentleman and went around the corner to William Street. We waited a couple of minutes and then an enormous blast took place. Windows were blown out and Belgian blocks were ripped out of the street. This was no firecracker, but a stick of dynamite.

As Easter came many of us bought new suits. This was a tradition at the time because when we went to church, or had an occasion, even a dance, we would wear a suit. This particular year was different. The fashion mode changed, as peg pants and padded shoulders were the fad. We all had our own favorite stores to purchase a suit. Those of us who had limited funds went to Delancy Street to *Moe Levy's, Robert Hall,* or *Howard's.* For the near well-to-do there was *Joe Friedman* or *Rogers Peet.* On Easter, I went to church with my family and later on caught up with my friends. My first sighting was Eugene B. in a solid dark suit bought at *Rogers Peet.* Next appeared Mickey and Jamsie in sharp grey suits. I had a silver plaid suit. Paulie G., however, was conspicuously missing, most likely visiting numerous cousins and friends for Easter. Suddenly, on this bright Sunday afternoon a shout was heard from the corner of William and Pearl streets. We had all gathered near Augrick's admiring our outfits. We all looked and there was Paulie in a chartreuse, one-button suit peppered with orange raindrops. We all looked in awe as we saw this extremely good-looking Italian kid standing on the corner, resplendent in this amazing colorful suit, 16 peg, huge shoulders, drenched in sunlight. What a sight to behold. Only in America!

Chapter Thirty-five

Despite severe monetary shortfalls, we always seemed to have enough money for food. No. 16 Mott Street in Chinatown was a favorite place for the local neighborhood gentry. There the maitre d', Larry, always provided bread to those who requested it. There was your *Club Diner* on James Street, *Katz's* on Houston Street for deli, but our favorite was *Forlini's*, located at No. 5 Baxter Street, and then 93 Baxter. Mr. Forlini, the father, was a very personable man who had a great rapport with his customers. His three sons, Frank, Freddie, and Hugo, all emigrated from Italy and worked for their father—one a cook, another a bartender, and the third a waiter. All of the sons and their father worked long and hard hours. What a pleasure to order a hot roast beef sandwich with gravy and French fries for seventy-five cents. Their menu was full of hearty and tasty meals, including their hot antipasto, polenta, risotto, and osso buco.

The Forlinis always represented the American dream. All came here very poor with no English language skills. They worked sixty to seventy hours a week doing their best to raise their families. They had little time to enjoy themselves. Their lives were for others, their motives lacking any form of selfishness. The business built day by day grew every year. They all spoke fluent English and served their country in the armed forces. Frank was a decorated paratrooper in World War II. To me, the Forlinis were the classic example of the fulfillment of why our families came to this country. They loved this country and, while enriching themselves, they built a better nation.

The sons opened their business together after No. 5 Baxter Street was torn down. Today their succeeding generations run the business. The Forlinis established themselves in our neighborhood as icons, and there was much to admire in this family. Their success made us all proud, but also provided a wonderful establishment for eating delicious home-style food.

Chapter Thirty-six

The neighborhood was about to change again. We, as a group of friends, were about to dissipate; a catastrophic event was about to take place. We were all notified that a huge cooperative housing project called Chatham Green would be built. Our homes would be condemned and demolished. Our beautiful church, St. Joachim, would also be torn down. In addition, parts of Pearl Street from Park Row to Chambers Street to City Hall would be destroyed, to make way for a new police headquarters.

I sat down with my father and mother and my much younger sister and brother. Where would we go? Our four hundred sq. ft. apartment gave us so much joy and warmth. It was a place to rest, to eat, and to talk. Our family always engaged in conversation with great joy.

Paul and I stood on the corner of Madison and Roosevelt streets. I had my arm around Paul's shoulder, and as we looked down Roosevelt Street our eyes welled with tears. All of our memories and precious moments were now before us. Our elected and local officials, who had always served themselves better than their constituents, had let us down again. Was this an exercise in eminent domain or a wanton disregard for the wonderful people who occupied these streets? From Chambers to St. James Place to Chatham Square to City Hall...all these buildings were to be destroyed in the name of progress and, of course, greed and selfishness. A tragedy of major proportion was about to unfold. Paul and I were about to join the army; my mother was now dying of cancer. All the boys who were fortunate to return to their homes from the War were now ripped away by callous officials who once before had destroyed our neighborhood by constructing low-income housing that became superslums. To think that the local Democratic Party objected to our softball uniforms because we used Al Smith rather than Alfred E. Smith, but did not raise a whimper when news of the demolition was announced. I was sure Governor Al Smith had turned over in his grave because of this inaction.

The 1960s were fast approaching. It seemed that many things besides our neighborhood were changing. Another war was about to begin. Drug use was becoming more commonplace. It seemed that the next decade would witness a social upheaval, which it did. Paul and I returned from the service and our families had relocated to new homes—Paul's family was in Queens and mine was in Yonkers, where my Uncle Jim built a new home for my family. The enjoyment did not take place, as my mother passed away in 1960 at the age of forty-nine. The closest human being I had known was gone. It seemed that a future life could never give me the happiness and joy of a young boy running around those historic streets of New York City, filled with dreams and hope. The pressures of life had always seemed contained. The joy of the future piqued our interest. We grew up naturally, with the reinforcement of love from our families, the solid philosophy of a good education, and hard work. The traditional values of American life were slowly dissipating, indicating the beginning of the end of life, as we knew it. The life *between two bridges* was now a memory, albeit a beautiful one.

THE END

LIST OF NEIGHBORHOOD NICKNAMES

Butch
Joe I to Joe XII
Goo-Goo
Quey
Richie Comb
Bobby Punk
Bobo the Hippo
Jimmey Brute
Mickey Mouse
Paulie Batman
Victor Star
Pete the Lash
Louie Fox
Cheese
Johnny Black
Jeannie Black
Bobby Costy
Frankie Bull I to Frankie Bull III
Richie Igor
Roger Monk
Eugene Brow
Hammerhead
Boobsy
Red
Bunney

Freddy Baloney
Bucky
Billy Ga Ding Ding
Joe Oakie
Rocky Nails
Johnny One Eye
Jimmey No Eyes
Mooney
Dumbo
Georgie Egg
Murphy
Doc
Manny Bull
Pepe
Jackie Fat
Dapper
Paulie Knock-knock
Johnny Tra Chi Mor
Bopo
Bimbo
Johnny Turkey
Jimmey Cricket
Danny Fat
Carlo Gimp
Carlo Head
Junior

Raymond Rotsie
Ray Bug
Frankie Molach
Avelino
Waacky
Washey
    If I forgot you, please forgive me

CPSIA information can be obtained at www.ICGtesting.com
Printed in the USA
BVOW021033280213

314422BV00011B/203/P